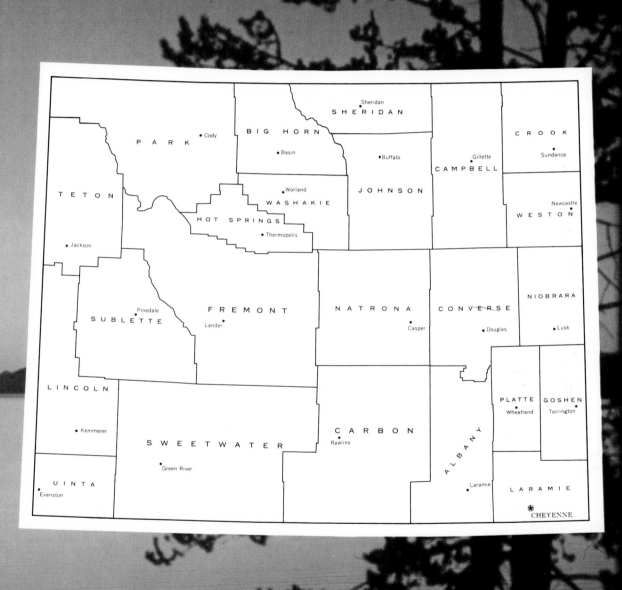

PARK   • Cody

BIG HORN   • Basin

Sheridan •
SHERIDAN

CROOK   • Sundance

TETON

JOHNSON   • Buffalo

CAMPBELL   • Gillette

WASHAKIE   • Worland

HOT SPRINGS   • Thermopolis

• Jackson

WESTON   • Newcastle

SUBLETTE   • Pinedale

FREMONT   • Lander

NATRONA   • Casper

CONVERSE   • Douglas

NIOBRARA   • Lusk

LINCOLN   • Kemmerer

SWEETWATER   • Green River

CARBON   • Rawlins

ALBANY   • Laramie

PLATTE   • Wheatland

GOSHEN   • Torrington

UINTA   • Evanston

LARAMIE

⊛ CHEYENNE

The New
Enchantment of America
WYOMING

By Allan Carpenter

 CHILDRENS PRESS, CHICAGO

ACKNOWLEDGMENTS

For assistance in the preparation of the revised edition, the author thanks:
PAULA WEST, Wyoming State Archives and Historical Department; and Wyoming Travel Commission.

American Airlines—Anne Vitaliano, Director of Public Relations; *Capitol Historical Society*, Washington, D.C.; *Newberry Library,* Chicago, Dr. Lawrence Towner, Director; *Northwestern University Library*, Evanston, Illinois; *United Airlines*—John P. Grember, Manager of Special Promotions; Joseph P. Hopkins, Manager, News Bureau; Carl Provorse, *Carpenter Publishing House.*

UNITED STATES GOVERNMENT AGENCIES: *Department of Agriculture*—Robert Hailstock, Jr., Photography Division, Office of Communication; Donald C. Schuhart, Information Division, Soil Conservation Service. *Army*—Doran Topolosky, Public Affairs Office, Chief of Engineers, Corps of Engineers. *Department of Interior*—Louis Churchville, Director of Communications; EROS Space Program—Phillis Wiepking, Community Affairs; Charles Withington, Geologist; Mrs. Ruth Herbert, Information Specialist; Bureau of Reclamation; National Park Service—Fred Bell and the individual sites; Fish and Wildlife Service—Bob Hines, Public Affairs Office. *Library of Congress*—Dr. Alan Fern, Director of the Department of Research; Sara Wallace, Director of Publications; Dr. Walter W. Ristow, Chief, Geography and Map Division; Herbert Sandborn, Exhibits Officer. *National Archives*—Dr. James B. Rhoads, Archivist of the United States; Albert Meisel, Assistant Archivist for Educational Programs; David Eggenberger, Publications Director; Bill Leary, Still Picture Reference; James Moore, Audio-Visual Archives. *United States Postal Service*—Herb Harris, Stamps Division.

For assistance in the preparation of the first edition, the author thanks:
Consultant Dorris L. Sanders, Director for Elementary Education for the State of Wyoming; Cecil Shaw, State Superintendent of Schools; T.H. Broad, Assistant Superintendent, Division of Instruction, Wyoming Department of Education; J.A. (Buck) Buchanan, Executive Director, Wyoming Natural Resource Board; and Karl G. Harper, News Editor, University of Wyoming.

Illustrations on the preceding pages:
Cover photograph: The Teton Range and the Snake River, USDI, NPS, Grand Teton National Park
Page 1: Commemorative stamps of historic interest
Pages 2-3: Yellowstone Lake at Sunrise, Wyoming Travel Commission
Page 3: (Map) USDI Geological Survey
Pages 4-5: Yellowstone National Park, EROS Space Photo, USDI Geological Survey, EROS Data Center

Project Editor, Revised Edition:
  Joan Downing
Assistant Editor, Revised Edition:
  Mary Reidy

Library of Congress Cataloging in Publication Data

Carpenter, John Allan, 1917-
  Wyoming.

  (His The new enchantment of America)
  Includes index.
  Edition of 1966 published under title: Wyoming, from its glorious past to the present.
  SUMMARY: Presents the geography and history of Wyoming and discusses its natural treasures, famous citizens, and scenic attractions.
  1. Wyoming—Juvenile literature.
[1. Wyoming] I. Title. II. Series.
F761.3.C3 1979   978.7   78-32135
ISBN 0-516-04150-9

2 3 4 5 6 7 8 9 10 11 12 R 85 84 83 82 81 80 79

Contents

A TRUE STORY TO SET THE SCENE 9
A Wilderness of Trouble

LAY OF THE LAND 13
Waters: Mirrored and Flowing—Lifting Their Heads to Heaven—Basins
and Valleys—Other Natural Features—In Ancient Times—Dry Bones:
Those Dry Bones—Climate

FOOTSTEPS ON THE LAND . . . . "Colter's Hell"—Other Early
Birds—Explorers and Emigrants—Relations with the Indians—Gleaming
Rails and Uproarious Towns

YESTERDAY AND TODAY 41
Congress Recognizes a Wonderland—Last Stand—Cattle Country—Tam-
ing the "Wild West"—A More Settled State

NATURAL TREASURES 53
Animals: One Apiece—Flying and Swimming—Growing Things—Mineral
Wealth—Water of Life

THE PEOPLE USE THEIR TREASURES 59
Minerals—Transportation and Communication—Other Activities

HUMAN TREASURES 63
Masters of the Frontier—Indian Chiefs—Notable Women—Creative People—Such Interesting People

TEACHING AND LEARNING 71

ENCHANTMENT OF WYOMING 73
Where Nature Comes to a Boil—"Sheer Majesty"—Other Northwest
Attractions—The Southwest—The Northeast—The Southeast

HANDY REFERENCE SECTION 89
Instant Facts—You Have a Date with History—Governors of Wyoming—
Thinkers, Doers, Fighters

INDEX 92

PICTURE CREDITS 96

ABOUT THE AUTHOR 96

Old Faithful has hardly changed since George Cowan's adventures.

A True Story to Set the Scene

A WILDERNESS OF TROUBLE

George F. Cowan lay where the Indians had left him for dead, with a bullet wound in the thigh and one on the head. He was also terribly bruised by rocks they had thrown at him. Suddenly this "corpse" recovered consciousness with a shudder, and Cowan managed to pull himself to his knees. After he had examined himself, he decided there might still be hope, and in this way began one of the strangest and most thrilling sagas in the history of the West.

Much that is or was typical of Wyoming is involved in this story. It includes a group of tourists, the wonders of Yellowstone, hostile Indians, wilderness adventure, great personal bravery, and last-minute rescue.

Cowan, his wife, and the rest of their party from Radersburg, Montana, had the misfortune to visit Yellowstone Park in 1877. They met the Nez Percé group of the great Chief Joseph, the younger, from Oregon. Joseph was leading his people to Canada in an effort to escape capture by United States soldiers. The Indians had swung as far south as Yellowstone to avoid settled regions.

Joseph had been proud that up to this time his group had never taken the life of a settler. The chief still spared the civilians he met and often even bought their supplies rather than capturing them. At their camp not far from Fountain Geyser, the Cowans were captured by Joseph and his group. Later the chief gave them their freedom. However, a group of braves returned after the chiefs were out of sight, captured or drove off the other members of the party and left Cowan for dead. They then moved on with Mrs. Cowan and the other captives.

Cowan had scarcely drawn himself up after recovering consciousness when another Indian spotted him and shot him in the back, again leaving him for dead. Finding himself still able to crawl on his knees, Cowan started out, without food or water, now suffering from three bullet wounds and severe bruises—on a journey "which probably has no parallel in history."

He crawled from dusk till midnight until he came upon a sleeping Indian and had to make a wide detour around him. He found a group of lame horses, abandoned by the Indians, but he could not get to any of them. He went on for several days in this agonizingly slow, painful way until he reached the wagons the Indians had forced his party to abandon some days before. No food was left there, but one of the company's bird dogs was still there. She rushed to attack him but recognized him in time and went into frenzies of joy to see him.

Next Cowan reached their old camp, near Fountain Geyser, where he found a few grains of coffee and several matches. He managed to make some coffee in an old fruit can, and this was his first nourishment of any kind since the attack.

After resting overnight, he and the dog started out again, heading for a spot on Nez Percé Creek where he thought he might be rescued. Suddenly he saw two men who, to his great joy, turned out to be men from the army, sent out to find his body and bury it.

They built a large fire, gave him food, and left him to wait for the rest of the army to come by and carry him to safety. Misfortune continued to plague him. He went to sleep and soon woke to find himself trapped by a fierce fire burning in the vegetable mold that surrounded him. He managed to escape after suffering severe burns.

At last the rest of the army came up, took him to camp, and treated his wounds and burns. He was placed in a wagon when the army moved on. Suddenly he found himself deserted and thought the army had abandoned him. However, they soon came back to explain they had gone out to meet an expected Indian attack, but found they were friendly Indians. They left Cowan at Bottler's ranch, just outside the northern boundary of Yellowstone.

Mrs. Cowan, who had gotten safely away from the Indians after much difficulty, finally learned where her husband was and came with a wagon for him. Still following his trail of bad luck, the team broke away on a steep slope and the wagon overturned. Only the great amount of bedding saved him from more serious injury. When a man with a horse happened by, he helped get the wagon to Fort Ellis, and they finally got an ambulance wagon to take them to Bozeman, Montana, where Cowan found a hotel room.

Wyoming geology is strikingly illustrated in this sandstone with festoon cross-bedding of the Casper formation south of Laramie.

Cowan lay quietly on his bed while more and more of his friends gathered to hear his story and congratulate him on such a miraculous escape. So many sat on his bed that the bed collapsed in a wreck on the floor, fortunately without hurting him. The hotel owner jokingly said he would have to ask him to leave, since he could hardly afford to have such an unlucky person around.

In spite of all his troubles, George Cowan recovered and lived to a ripe old age. In 1901, twenty-four years after his great adventure, he returned to Yellowstone to visit the locations where he had such desperate times. Hiram Chittenden, who was with him then, wrote, "His recollection of localities was astonishingly vivid and accurate."

Lime Terrace in Hot Springs Park.

12

Lay of the Land

"When I ask my Great Spirit to take care of me, when I am through with this world, I do not ask for harps, haloes, wings or white robes.... But I ask Him for a good camping place in a beautiful valley like one of those in Wyoming where I might stay through all eternity." The speaker was Wyoming pioneer J.D. Woodruff. His feeling about the sweeping plains, soaring mountains, crystal-aired valleys, and sun-drenched plateaus would still be echoed by most of the residents of Wyoming.

They might have been willing to "string up" the great American statesman Daniel Webster when he mistakenly declared in 1844 that the land now called Wyoming "was not worth a cent ... a region of savages, wild beasts, shifting sands, whirlwinds of dust, cactus."

The savages are gone; the wild beasts are still one of the great attractions, and there might still be found a few shifting sands, dust eddies, and some blooming cactus. But to the America of today the state where the Great Plains meet the Rocky Mountains offers much, much more.

In a sense it is a "man-made" state—a perfect rectangle with no "natural" features such as rivers and oceans to form its boundaries. In all the country there are only four states with completely artificial boundaries. It is the only state made up of territory from each of the four great territories annexed by the United States west of the Mississippi—Louisiana Purchase, Texas annexation, Oregon Territory, and territory added as a result of the Mexican War.

Wyoming is a huge plateau broken by craggy, pine-clad mountains and indented by basins and valleys. Across the state writhes the mighty backbone of the United States—the Continental Divide. East of the divide, the land slopes downward, generally, to the east and north.

Few features of geography have the romantic appeal of the great watersheds or divides, and the divides in Wyoming are unique in many ways. Two Ocean Pass, just south of Yellowstone Park, has been called "the most remarkable example of such phenomena in the world." Atlantic Creek and Pacific Creek form less than a quarter of a mile (.4 kilometer) apart, and yet their waters reach the two mighty oceans separated by many thousands of miles. At high water, water flowing from a canyon separates at exactly the crest of the divide and flows into each of the two creeks. Waters of Isa Lake in Yellowstone Park drain into both the Atlantic and Pacific oceans.

In other parts of Wyoming, the waters are even farther divided. Near Dubois is a three-way watershed. From this point some waters flow to the Atlantic through the Missouri River system, some to the Pacific through the Snake and Columbia river system and some to the Gulf of California through the Green and Colorado river system.

WATERS: MIRRORED AND FLOWING

In dry Wyoming it may seem surprising that there are 20,000 miles (32,187 kilometers) of streams. Ten rivers flowing in Wyoming are listed by the United States Geological Survey among the major rivers of the country: Green, North Platte, Yellowstone, Snake, Bighorn, Powder, Little Missouri, Niobrara, Cheyenne, and Tongue.

Some of Wyoming's rivers are among the most storied and romantic of the West. In fact, the Powder River has been called "the stream that has come to symbolize the West." Another romantic stream, the Wind River, suddenly changes its name and becomes the Bighorn River.

The Green, the Snake, and the Yellowstone, three of the mightiest in the nation, have their beginnings in Wyoming. The Green begins in the Green River Lakes northwest of Gannett Peak, the Snake north of the south boundary of Yellowstone Park, and the Yellowstone River just south of that boundary. The eccentric Bear River, which flows north, west, and south, crosses state boundaries at six places in its erratic course. Flowing into Great Salt Lake, it is the longest river of the country not having an outlet to the ocean.

In northern Wyoming, the greatest watercourse was called by the Indians the "River of the Yellow Stone," because of the unusual color of the great canyon it had cut through that yellow stone. We know their river as the Yellowstone yet today. The North Platte has been called "too yellow to wash with and too pale to paint with," because of the volume of light-colored soil it carries.

The Popo Agie ranks among the more unusual of the country's many disappearing rivers. One of its branches disappears into a sink on the side of a mountain near Lander. Then, below, it bursts out and tumbles over a waterfall. Another of the historic rivers of Wyoming is the Laramie.

Natural and artificial bodies of water dot Wyoming to a surprising extent. The largest lake on the North American continent at an altitude of over 7,500 feet (2,286 meters) is Yellowstone Lake. It is 300 feet (91.4 meters) deep at its deepest point. The second largest natural lake in the state is Jackson Lake, one of the world's most beautiful and most photographed lakes. Many small nearby lakes nestle in the Teton Mountains. Jewellike Jenny and Leigh lakes are beloved of everyone who visits the region.

Bull Lake, near Crowheart, was known to the Indians as "The Lake that Roars." Legends told of the rare white buffalo bull driven into the lake and drowned by Indian hunters who wanted his white robe. Wind catches under the ice, raises it a little, and then lets the ice drop, with a sighing moan. This is said by the legend to be the angry roar of the white buffalo's spirit.

Another Wyoming lake of legend is Lake De Smet, south of Sheridan. Stories of the lake tell of the horrible monster that sometimes rises from its mists and also of the tragic Indian maiden, Star Dust, who drowned in the lake and whose false lover forever calls out to her in the moaning voice of the wind.

Other natural Wyoming lakes include Cooper, James, Fremont, and Hattie. Most of the mountains of Wyoming cradle many sparkling lakes, such as Mirror, Silver, and Marie in the Snowy Range.

Many giant dams have tamed the raging rivers of Wyoming and stored their water as an invaluable treasure of the arid regions. Although Flaming Gorge Dam is in Utah, most of the mighty lake it impounds stretches north along the Green River valley into Wyoming. Other major dams and lakes include Pathfinder, Seminoe, Alcova, Boysen, Glendo, Keyhole, Big Sandy, Buffalo Bill (Shoshone), Wheatland, and Guernsey.

Early water reclamation efforts are shown in this painting of Buffalo Bill Dam by Edward Laning, commissioned by the Bureau of Reclamation, USDI.

LIFTING THEIR HEADS TO HEAVEN

The many mountain ranges and their numerous subdivisions help to make Wyoming truly a mountain state.

Major mountain ranges of Wyoming include Laramie Range, east and north of Laramie, cresting in Laramie Peak, 10,272 feet (3,131 meters); Bighorn Mountains, with Cloud Peak at 13,175 feet (4,016 meters); the Snowy (or Medicine Bow) Range, topped by Medicine Bow Peak, 12,013 feet (3,662 meters); and the Absaroka Range, with Ptarmigan Mountain at 12,250 feet (3,734 meters) as its highest point. The most lofty point in Wyoming is Gannett Peak, 13,785 feet (4,202 meters), in the extensive Wind River Range. Almost as elevated is the 13,766 feet (4,196 meters) craggy pinnacle of Grand Teton in the Teton Range.

16

Some of the many subdivisions of these ranges and other independent small ranges are the Gros Ventre, Sierra Madre, Seminoe, Wapiti, Tump, Salt River, and in the far northeast even a portion of the Black Hills, known as the Black Hills of Wyoming. Although the latter only reach a maximum height of 6,673 feet (2,034 meters) in Wyoming, almost anywhere else they would be considered very sizeable mountains.

BASINS AND VALLEYS

The Continental Divide wanders crazily across the country, but in Wyoming is one of its most unusual features. It splits into two parts and spreads these two arms around what is called the Great Divide Basin. This is a bowl-shaped plateau from which no waters flow to any ocean. Part of this region is known as the Red Desert.

Small parts of Wyoming on the border west of Bear River Divide lie in America's Great Basin that includes much of Utah, most of Nevada, and portions of Idaho and Oregon. Streams that flow into this region have no outlet to the sea but end in desert sinks, in salt lakes, or even in freshwater lakes with no visible outlets.

Mt. Moran in Grand Teton National Park.

The Lower Falls of the Yellowstone River.

Other Wyoming basins, such as Bighorn, have mighty outlets to the ocean, like the Bighorn River.

Some of the nation's best-known and most spectacular valleys are gouged out of the Wyoming plains and mountains. Jackson Hole has become one of the world's best-known valleys. At its widest, Jackson Hole is about 12 miles (19.3 kilometers), and it crouches for 60 miles (96.5 kilometers) along the base of the Teton Mountains. One of the reasons for the almost overwhelming majesty of the Tetons is the fact that they rise abruptly from Jackson Hole without any foothills.

Sheridan Valley, 15 miles (24.1 kilometers) wide and 30 miles (48.3 kilometers) long, is another of the larger valleys.

Wyoming is a land of mighty canyons. Not very many miles from its source, beginning at Alpine Junction, the Snake River has carved its Grand Canyon, the first of the awesome gorges of this amazing river. Even more awesome and one of the best-known works of nature is the Grand Canyon of the Yellowstone. The many varying golden colors of the walls of this canyon are unique in the world.

Tensleep Creek has carved deep and rugged Tensleep Canyon. Like Yellowstone, Shell Canyon has the added attraction of a falls at its head. Flaming Gorge offers one of the most scenic drives in the nation. Rainbow Canyon of the Badlands offers canyon country of still another type.

Through the great ramparts of lava and other rocks that form a wall around Yellowstone to the east, the only break is Shoshone Canyon. Another mighty cleft in the rocks is Wind River Canyon, piercing the Owl Creek Range, with 2,000-foot (609.6-meter) cliffs of black diorite rock. North of Lamont, Devils Gate, 330 feet (100.5 meters) deep and only 30 feet (9.1 meters) wide at the bottom, has been called "one of the most notable features of its kind in the world." The narrows of the Snake River are 3,000 feet (914.4 meters) deep, in places only 40 feet (12.2 meters) wide, and the river rushes through with a roar that can be heard for miles.

OTHER NATURAL FEATURES

Satan has been responsible for the names of many striking features of the Wyoming country. In addition to Devils Gate, Devils Tower rises 1,280 feet (390 meters) above the Belle Fourche River, soaring almost straight up for its last 865 feet (263.7 meters). Hell's Half Acre, near Waltman, is an area of weird rock formations and eroded canyons, always held in awe by the Indians.

Castle Gardens offers strange formations—red spires and toadstools supported on slender stems. Independence Rock has been called "one of the most significant erosion remnants in the West." Church Buttes near Fort Bridger thrust themselves out of stony ground where they make a landmark visible for miles around.

One of the great remaining primitive areas is the Wind River Wilderness along the east slopes of that range. In the Wind River Glacier region, also, some of the finest glaciers are to be found.

Less picturesque but occupying huge areas of the state are the enormous plains regions of Wyoming, the Central Northern Plains, the Laramie Plains, and other plateau and plains lands. Southeast of Douglas is a typical badlands region, and there is an area of great sand dunes near Rock Springs.

IN ANCIENT TIMES

During the many millions of years of earth's history in Wyoming, oceans have come and gone. Mountains have pushed themselves up only to be slowly eroded and then sometimes to push themselves up again. Ancient tiny creatures left their colorful bodies to build up coral reefs. Seas have come and gone. Prehistoric volcanoes have sent forth outpourings of lava and volcanic ash. Sediment pouring down the slopes of mountains has filled the nearby basins and sometimes covered the mountains, only to have streams flow through more rapidly and wash the mountains bare again. Over the years, wind, rain, and streams in some places have cut through all the layers of rock, hardened lava, and coral reefs, to expose again all the various layers that tell the story of eons past in Wyoming.

One of the mightiest efforts of nature in Wyoming was the "epic Teton uplift." As if a giant hand were pushing them from below, the Tetons slowly rose in a great stone block, with the east face almost straight up. These are known as the "block-fault" type of mountains. The height to which these mountains were raised is shown by the fact that coral reefs from ancient seas have been found at the 10,000-foot (3048-meter) level.

The great glacier sheets of the Ice Ages did not cover Wyoming, but as the glaciers elsewhere made the climate colder, the mountain glaciers were enlarged until they covered most of the higher mountain ranges. As they pushed farther and farther down the slopes, they gouged out basins in the canyons and left deposits of rocks called moraines at their edges. When the glaciers melted and receded, the waters filled the basins, making "cirque" lakes, and backed behind the moraine dams forming still more mountain lakes. The glaciers sculptured the higher parts of the mountains into even more rugged peaks, such as the spire of Grand Teton.

Glaciers still remain on some of Wyoming's mountainsides. They gleam white in the deep crevices of the Tetons and blanket many a gully in Wind River Range.

When the older glaciers melted, the enormous amount of glacier water made many of the lakes much larger than they are now. Yellowstone Lake at one time was dammed by a glacier and was at least 160 feet (48.8 meters) deeper than it now is. At that time it drained into the Pacific instead of the Atlantic.

When Yellowstone Lake at last burst through the dam of ice and earth holding it to the north and was reduced to its present size, the rush of water rapidly cut through the layers of yellow rock which had been partly broken up by hot water and vapor from below. This was the beginning of its Grand Canyon. It was formed in a relatively short period of time and is a "young" wonder compared to others of its type.

One of the best examples of volcanic action in Wyoming is marvelous Devils Tower. This was formed by what is called a molten rock intrusion. Rock heated so that it would flow like pastry dough was squeezed upward through an opening in the earth's crust, as if from a giant pastry tube. The beautiful Blue Holes, extinct geysers near Dubois, might indicate that the forces of heat beneath the earth's surface are diminishing.

DRY BONES: THOSE DRY BONES!

Wyoming is one of the world's great depositories of the preserved remains of ancient plants and animals—a kind of bank where deposits have been made that are of great value in our understanding of life on earth before written records were kept.

One of the most notable "withdrawals" from this "bank" was the famous "Horned Dinosaur" at Lance Creek. The Como Bluff dinosaur graveyard was discovered as early as 1877 and continues to yield fossils of the great reptiles.

Some of the finest and most perfect fossils of fishes have been found in Wyoming. West of Kemmerer and near Osage fossilized oyster, clam, and turtle, as well as fish, have been found.

Fossils of Wyoming range from the diggings near Rawlins of huge prehistoric mammoth to the dainty four-toed horse, or the crocodiles and doglike animals found among the fossils of Polecat Bench near Powell. The town of Fossil takes its name from the nearby fossil cliffs.

Near Medicine Bow is a petrified forest. Some of the trees that have been turned to stone here are of a semi-tropical type showing that the now dry land once was probably moist and steaming.

CLIMATE

Precipitation in Wyoming on a statewide average is 14.8 inches (about 376 millimeters) per year. Extremes of temperature are somewhat less difficult to endure because of the dry climate and high general elevation. The Yellowstone region is noted for its enormous snowfalls, and Hiland is said to be "notorious" for its blizzards. Winds of 70 and 80 miles (112.6 and 128.7 kilometers) per hour drive the snow across the plains until visibility is zero and all life outdoors is endangered. However, Lander has the lowest wind velocity of any city in the United States, with Sheridan second.

The drying Chinook winds that sweep over the Rockies have been known to melt deep snowbanks as in a blast from a furnace. Visitors who wonder at the need for bridges over dry stream beds will be told that they are in cloudburst country. The rare heavy rains quickly fill the valleys and send raging torrents down gullies, which ordinarily are dry as dust.

Among the finest of climates is that of the Green River Valley, where the mountains provide shelter from extremes of temperature. Winters are mild and summer heat is moderate.

Footsteps on the Land

PEOPLE OF MYSTERY

Although people are known to have lived in Wyoming for twelve thousand or perhaps as long as twenty thousand years, very little is really known about the ancient peoples there.

One of the world's most fascinating prehistoric relics is found in Wyoming. This is the mysterious Medicine Wheel, on the top of Medicine Mountain in the Bighorns, west of Sheridan. The wheel is formed by huge rocks laid in a circumference of 245 feet (74.6 meters). From a center cairn stone, 28 stone spokes radiate. Around the rim of the wheel are six crude rock shelters, or shrines, now called medicine tepees. It is thought that medicine men may have huddled there during ancient religious rites. A seventh medicine tepee stands about 15 feet (4.6 meters) away.

Various authorities are amazed by the similar appearance of this wheel with one in the Gobi Desert, and also with the famous ruin at Stonehenge in England. However, at the moment no way is known in which these three widely separated works could possibly have any association with one another.

The Wyoming Medicine Wheel was long known to the Indians. They had no idea what it was, but they guessed that it had something to do with religion. For this reason, apparently, it was visited by great numbers of Indians, and the marks of their *travois* can still be seen. Even more of a puzzle is the great 58-foot (17.7-meter) arrow made of rocks with an arrowhead 5 feet (1.5 meters) across. This is laid on the ground not far from Meeteetse. Strangely, it points directly at the Medicine Wheel far across the Bighorn Basin.

Another mystery is the "rude granite structure on the top of Grand Teton," which is thought to be very ancient.

Prehistoric cooking pots, giant pestles, and other relics of ancient peoples have been found in Wyoming, but no prehistoric metal tools. At a prehistoric campsite not far from Church Buttes, choppers, points, scrapers, and quartzite blades were found, unexplainably identical to others found in Europe and Africa.

The prehistoric pictographs (painted) and petroglyphs (carved) on rocks and cliffs are common. The most skillful of these seem to be the pictographs of Castle Gardens. Those near Shoshoni seem to show Europeans, and it is thought that these may have been Spaniards who in some way were known to the artists. Some of the Wyoming pictographs are of the rare, red-painted type, and some are found so high up on cliffs that it is impossible to guess how the artists ever reached the spot.

South of Manville are the mysterious "Spanish Diggings." These stone quarries may be from two hundred fifty to five thousand years old. Early explorers thought the quarries had been worked by Spaniards, but this is now not considered probable. However, it is difficult to explain such items as the 60-foot (18.3-meter) stone cross found in the quarries. Hammers, grinders, axes, knives, and other implements, all of stone, have been found in the diggings. Identical instruments have been turned up in prehistoric mounds as far away as the Ohio and Mississippi valleys.

MANY SLEEPS AGO

In several parts of Wyoming even today are found circles of flat stones. These were tepee rings used by the Indians to hold the edges of their buffalo hide tepees to the ground. They remain as reminders of the twelve mighty groups that used to rule the land of Wyoming.

Most of the Indians found when Europeans first went into Wyoming had been there only a comparatively short time. The Crows were the earliest Indian people known in the region. Gradually they were pushed out by Arikara, Arapaho, Bannock, Blackfoot, Cheyenne, Flathead, Gros Ventre, Kiowa, Modoc, Nez Percé, Shoshone, Sioux, and Ute.

For some reason these groups avoided the region of Yellowstone Park. It is usually thought that the steaming and boiling forces there kept the superstitious Indians away. More likely they just did not find it to be a very good place. Only the Sheepeater group is known to have lived in the Yellowstone region. Sheepeater people have

Indians Attacking the Grizzly Bear, *by Currier and Ives.*

been called "pitiful, timorous creatures," who made only the crudest shelters, wore almost no clothing, and often were forced to live on a diet of grasshoppers and ants. However, other authorities have said, "As a rule they were intelligent and self-reliant people."

Most of the Indians of Wyoming had moderate skill in making things with their hands. Each group could be recognized by the distinctive pattern and decoration of its tepees. Rawhide shields were often highly decorated. War bonnets served the same purpose as modern-day medals, each feather representing a battle honor. The Indians made skin cradles and parfleches, a decorated skin bag; where soapstone quarries were available, such as at Torrey Lake, they carved soapstone dishes and smoking pipes. Coiled pottery was also fairly common.

In the volcanic regions, obsidian provided material for shiny arrowheads of real glass. Many groups made fine snowshoes, a necessity in regions where snows were sometimes 15 feet (4.6 meters) deep. Brilliant red and yellow clays were smeared on as body paint, in frightening designs. Distances were measured in the number of nights or "sleeps" it took to reach a certain place. The town of Tensleep got its distinctive name because it was "ten sleeps" away from both Fort Laramie and Yellowstone.

The greatest wealth of the plains Indians was in their horses. These, of course, had come into the region only since some had been left in the southwest by early Spaniards. One of the greatest accomplishments of a young Indian brave was to steal or forcefully take away another's horse. Taking of scalps was another way of proving bravery.

The Sioux had come originally from forest lands to the east. When they went west it was said they "became the most formidable mounted warriors in America." A large part of the Black Hills in both Wyoming and South Dakota was considered sacred by the Sioux. They had strong feeling for the land and for their religious rites. The Sun Dance was an annual event of great religious significance.

The Sun Dance in different forms was recognized as one of the principal rites of the Arapaho and Shoshone, also.

One writer has said that the Indians "built an entire way of life around the huge herds of shaggy buffalo, relying on them for food, clothing, shelter, and as an object of religious worship. They hunted fleet antelope and graceful deer and they were seldom hungry. They lived unhurried and uncluttered lives and were in peaceful harmony with the beauties of nature that surrounded them."

"COLTER'S HELL"

No one knows just when the first explorers visited Wyoming. Some of the Spanish expeditions in the 1500s or 1600s may have touched the area. A Jesuit map of 1792 has a correct sketch of the Black Hills and Bighorn Mountains, and the information to make this must have come at a much earlier date. Some early ruins, forts, and relics may have been left by early Spaniards, but this may never be known accurately.

The famous French Vérendrye brothers are often said to have been the first Europeans in Wyoming, but now it is felt that they only came in sight of the Bighorns on their trapping and exploring expeditions.

The first European known to have touched Wyoming was John Colter—one of the most unusual men of our history. Colter kept no diaries or written records, and the accounts of others who talked with him or who knew him are often contradictory. Consequently, not much is known accurately about his life.

Colter was working for the trader Manuel Lisa, who had set up his post at the mouth of the Bighorn River. Lisa sent Colter south and west to tell the Indians that the new trading post was operating and to urge them to bring in their best furs for trading.

Of course, John Colter is best known as the discoverer of Yellowstone Park. Yellowstone is usually thought of as the region called "Colter's Hell." Strangely enough, according to Burton Harris, Colter's Hell was not Yellowstone, but was an area farther to the east, now covered by Buffalo Bill Reservoir.

This was the first discovery of thermal activity made by Colter, where he said he found hot springs, geysers, pools of scalding water, and a spring bubbling with tar. When he described what he had seen, he also added flames shooting from the ground. Either he was trying to make an impression or the great clouds of escaping steam had seemed like flame.

Later Colter continued his travels in a great loop around northwestern Wyoming. He was the first European known to see the Tetons and to discover Teton Pass. Then came the wonders of Yellowstone, somewhat dimmed for him by what he had seen previously in "Colter's Hell." Then he returned to Lisa's fort.

When Colter described the wonders he had seen, probably adding a good deal to the truth, he was laughed at and called a great liar. Many years were to go by before the public really knew about or believed in the amazing things that were first found in Wyoming by that extraordinary man, John Colter.

OTHER EARLY BIRDS

When John Jacob Astor established Astoria, his fur-trading post, at the mouth of the Columbia River in Oregon, the main party went

Emigrants Crossing the Plains, *by Currier and Ives.*

around South America by boat. However, Astor also sent a land party under the direction of Wilson Price Hunt. They crossed into Wyoming near the northeastern corner and took a zigzag course south and west and finally also went out over Teton Pass, after naming Hoback Canyon for trapper John Hoback.

Hunt's journey across this wilderness was the first ever taken by Europeans and it "brought Wyoming definitely into American history." Six months later, a small group returned from the Astor fort on the Columbia, led by Robert Stuart; they camped for the winter near present-day Bessemer Bend and Torrington. Their trail-blazing journey could really be said to have opened what later was known as the Oregon Trail. Among the other important things, they discovered the opening that came to be known as South Pass.

In 1822, General William H. Ashley set up a trading center on the Yellowstone River. He had new ideas for succeeding in fur trading and hired only trained horsemen who were also expert riflemen. Rather than set up trading posts throughout his wilderness empire, General Ashley decided to substitute an annual meeting of trappers, traders, Indians, and others who wanted to do business with him. This could be held in various convenient locations from year to year.

The first of these was rather small and was held in 1824 on the

Green River by Ashley's assistant, Thomas Fitzpatrick, known to the Indians as "Broken Hand, Chief of the Mountain Men." Ashley himself held the next meeting and called a rendezvous in 1825 near present-day Burntfork and McKinnon. The annual rendezvous, held until the 1840s, was a brawling, colorful event where the shelters of the Europeans were close to the striking-looking tepees of the Indians, who all came—men, women, and children, as well as dogs and horses. The various trading companies competed for furs and for the next year's services of the best trappers. Fortunes were made and lost. There were games, contests, and many fights. Sometimes there might be as many as one thousand five hundred people at a rendezvous—possibly more than the present-day population of the areas where they were held.

As the trappers spread out over the haunts of the fur-bearing animals, particularly the beaver, they began to know the secrets of the region—the locations of the streams, mountains, and other landmarks. Unfortunately, they kept no records, so these discoveries had to be made all over again by other explorers. Trapping was a lonesome, hard, and dangerous business. It is estimated that three-fifths of all the early trappers were killed by the Indians.

Only the hardiest and cleverest survived. Among the men who came with Ashley were several whose names became known throughout the country. These included Jim Bridger, Jim Beckwourth, William Sublette, and David E. Jackson. Jim Bridger visited Yellowstone at least as early as 1830. In later years he visited with a prominent editor about what he had seen in Yellowstone. The editor prepared a story on this but never printed it, fearing that people would refuse to believe that Bridger had really seen what he claimed. Later the editor publicly apologized to Bridger for not believing him.

Not until 1828 was the first true trading post set up in Wyoming, by Antonio Mateo, near the forks of Powder River. Hand-hewn logs were used to build a square stockade. Outside stood a huge press made of cottonwood. Here the beaver skins were tightly pressed into bales.

In 1829 William Sublette brought the first wheeled vehicles into Wyoming—ten wagons and two buggies. The great and famous expedition of Captain B.L.E. de Bonneville passed through Wyoming in 1832. His many wagons pressed the first tracks across Wyoming of the many to follow in the Oregon Trail.

Two missionaries, Dr. Marcus Whitman and the Reverend Samuel Parker, reached Wyoming in 1835, traveling with an American Fur Company party. At the head of Hoback Canyon in Wyoming, Reverend Parker preached what is thought to have been the first sermon delivered in present-day Wyoming — August 23, 1835.

Dr. Whitman returned to the East, and the next year came back through Wyoming, bringing his bride. With the Whitmans was another missionary, the Reverend Henry H. Spalding, also with his bride. These intrepid young ladies were the first white women known to have entered Wyoming.

In South Pass, in 1836, the Whitman party held the first Fourth of July celebration on the western slope of North America. Holding his Bible in one hand and clutching the flag of the United States in the other, Dr. Whitman prayed for the West as "a home of American mothers and the Church of Christ."

The Whitman party was just in time for the annual rendezvous of 1836. The trappers, amazed to see two white women, gave them an uproarious welcome. The Indians, even more astonished that such pale creatures could survive a trip of that length, gave them a great feast for which the fattest dogs were killed.

EXPLORERS AND EMIGRANTS

Although the trapping business was at its peak, the end was in sight, for it could not continue with the coming of "civilization" and the driving out of the fur-bearing animals. Already (in 1834) the first permanent settlement in present-day Wyoming had been established by Robert Campbell and William L. Sublette and sold two years later to the American Fur Company. They called it Fort William; later it came to be known as Fort John on the Laramie. When a shipping clerk left out "John on the" in addressing merchandise to the fort and called it simply Fort Laramie, the name sounded good, and that

Fort Laramie, 1834

became its name from then on—one of the most famous and important frontier outposts in all the West.

Most important of all the exploring parties to cross Wyoming was that of John C. Frémont in 1842. The timing was exactly right to interest the American people in the West. When he came to Fort Laramie, Frémont wrote, "Its lofty walls, whitewashed and picketed, with the large bastions at the angles ... with walls fifteen feet (4.6 meters) high. . . The great entrance was floored and about fifteen feet (4.6 meters) long; [it] made a pleasant, shaded seat through which the breeze swept constantly."

Frémont returned to Wyoming in 1843. While camped on the North Platte River near Rawlins, he built large wooden racks to dry the meat of many buffalo they had killed. This was cut in thin strips, hung on the racks and smoked. As they were busily smoking meat, they were attacked by a war party of seventy Arapaho and Cheyenne. After the attack had been beaten off, the Indians apologized, saying they thought the group was another Indian enemy war party. Then all smoked the peace pipe and exchanged gifts.

The second permanent settlement in Wyoming was begun in 1842 by frontiersman Jim Bridger, and it was named Fort Bridger in his honor. In the next year the first large-size group to cross the plains

31

passed Forts Laramie and Bridger on their way to Oregon by way of the route that, of course, became known as the Oregon Trail.

In 1849 Fort Laramie was bought by the United States as a military post. The primitive forts on the vast open spaces of Wyoming must have seemed like wonderful metropolises to weary travelers after untold miles of prairie, followed by mountains and plains. In the years after 1846, Mormons by the thousands made their way across the plains, seeking a place where they could be safe from persecution. At one time there were sixteen thousand Mormons traveling in Wyoming, the largest single migration in the country's history. The plains of Wyoming, known before to only a handful of frontiersmen and explorers, were crossed by two hundred thousand emigrants in the twenty years between 1843 and 1863.

In 1849 came the most incredible part of this mass movement of humanity—the rush to newly found gold in California. In 1850 alone an estimated sixty thousand people and ninety thousand domestic animals crossed Wyoming on the gold trail. As they pressed on faster and faster and grew ever more weary, they cast aside their precious belongings to lighten their loads. The trail was littered with crowbars, axes, trunks, anvils, wheels, wagons—and, sadly, the bones of animals and the graves of people who died along the way.

In the 1850s more Mormon groups passed through. This time they were mostly groups of poor people, coming all the way from Europe to reach their expected paradise in Utah. They had no wagon animals and had been provided with small carts that they pushed by hand across the weary miles. Two handcart companies were caught in early Wyoming blizzards and had a desperate time. A hundred Mormon pioneers died near Devils Gate during a period of nine days. Their bodies were buried in a single shallow trench, dug with great effort by the sorrowing survivors. Out of a thousand in these two handcart companies, almost two hundred died along the way. Among all the emigrant companies of the early days, it is estimated that the awful total of thirty-four thousand lost their lives on the trail.

A moving reminder of the thousands who made their tiresome, slow way across Wyoming is found in Register Cliff near Guernsey.

Here most of the travelers paused long enough to carve or scratch their names on the cliff, and many inscriptions can still be seen with their dates—some as early as 1842. Many found Warm Springs a wonderful natural place to wash their clothes, which became known as the Emigrants' Laundry Tub. This was a spring of abundant water flowing constantly at 70 degrees Fahrenheit (21.1 degrees Celsius).

At the strange, brooding formation known as Church Buttes, worship services were often held, while the emigrants paused on their way. It is interesting to picture a vesper service there as the sermon rang out across the vast and empty distances and the setting sun turned the whole west to crimson, throwing the enormously long butte into a looming black silhouette, while the first jewellike stars appeared in the incredibly clear sky of the silent Wyoming plains. Dim campfires and lanterns were the only lights to wink back at the stars. Today a bell on the summit still reminds travelers of the call to worship at the church of the plains.

As early as 1853 Mormons had pushed out from Utah to settle Fort Supply near Fort Bridger and Deer Creek, making these the first farming settlements in Wyoming. Later several other Mormon settlements were made in Wyoming, such as at Star Valley.

RELATIONS WITH THE INDIANS

Fort Laramie was the location of a great powwow of Indian groups with the United States Commissioners in 1851. A treaty was signed, in which the Indians agreed not to molest the wagon trains and to permit troops to be stationed along the trails for protection. The government promised to pay fifty thousand dollars per year to the Indians and guaranteed their traditional hunting grounds.

For three years both sides kept the bargain fairly well; the Sioux remained peaceful. Then August 19, 1854, an event occurred that according to one account was "the beginning of a war between the Plains Indians and the U.S. Army that lasted, almost without interruption, for thirty-five years."

It began when a Mormon emigrant complained to the commander

at Fort Laramie that a Sioux had stolen his cow. The commander sent Lieutenant John L. Grattan, with about thirty men, to bring in the cow thief. The Indians refused to surrender the offender, but they said they would bring him to the fort and surrender him themselves. If Grattan tried to use force, they warned that both he and his men would be killed. The interpreter was apparently intoxicated, and Grattan did not get the true meaning of what they said; mistakenly he ordered his troops to fire, and his men were massacred.

The period of greatest trouble with the Indians in Wyoming extended from 1862 to 1868. In 1865, five to six hundred Indians were massacred by governmental troops in Colorado, and the Indians throughout the West rose up in warfare. The year 1865 has been called the "bloody year" on the plains. Stagecoach stations and wagon trains were attacked almost constantly. Chief Red Cloud rallied the Indians to drive out the settlers. He became the "foremost chief of his time."

The government had pushed the "Bozeman Trail" through some of the richest Indian hunting lands and had built three forts—Reno, Phil Kearny, and C.F. Smith—to protect this trail to the gold fields of Montana. Red Cloud felt this was a direct violation of the treaty with the Indians. He especially hated Fort Kearny, and so many warriors

Taking the Back Track, *by Currier and Ives.*

were constantly prowling around there that only large and well-armed parties dared to go outside the walls.

On December 21, 1866, a wood-gathering party set out from Fort Kearny. Wood was available in the mountains about 5 miles (8 kilometers) distant. When word mistakenly came to the fort that the wood column had been attacked, Lieutenant Colonel W.J. Fetterman insisted that because he had seniority he should lead the rescue party from the fort. Unfortunately, he knew little about Indian fighting. He had boasted that given eighty men he could ride right through the middle of Red Cloud's warriors. He and his eighty-one men disappeared over a ridge; then shooting was heard. Captain Tenadore Ten Eyck took another seventy-six men to rescue Fetterman's party. Captain Ten Eyck described the scene: "One of our skirmishers in advance came back saying that what we supposed to be a heap of cottonwood logs was the bodies of Fetterman's men. This was true. All were killed. Within a small space most were found, horribly mutilated. I loaded the wagons with as many of the bodies as they could contain, being obliged to handle the greater part of them, the soldiers being so overcome with horror as almost unable to obey orders. It was after dark when we returned to the post."

The original firewood party came back safely, not knowing what had been going on.

With 2,500 painted angry warriors slinking around the fort on that bitter cold December evening, a scout and trader, John (Portugee) Phillips, volunteered to ride 237 miles (381.4 kilometers) to Fort Laramie for help. He asked for the commander's favorite thoroughbred horse, and slipped through the water gap in the stockade walls at midnight. For four days and nights horse and man existed on almost nothing, fought fear, deep snow drifts, and exhaustion, and arrived at Fort Laramie on Christmas night. Phillips interrupted a rousing Christmas night party with his message, and relief was soon on its way to Kearny. Portugee Phillips' accomplishment has been called "one of the truly heroic rides of American history."

The Fetterman massacre placed Red Cloud at the height of his power over his Sioux people and their Cheyenne allies. Not long afterward his scouts signaled with broken pieces of looking glass that another wood-gathering party was leaving the fort. The Indians did not know that a trap had been designed for them. This force was equipped with new rapid-fire rifles. Its commander, Captain James Powell, is said to have had iron plates fastened inside the bottoms of his wagons. When he reached the wood cutting grounds, he had the sixteen wagon boxes taken off the wheels and placed in a circle, forming a strong temporary fort.

The first wave of five hundred Sioux warriors, mounted on their best war ponies, charged the wagon-box barricade. A thousand more were ready to follow on foot. Captain Powell had a mere thirty-two men. He allowed the whooping Indians to come within 50 yards (45.7 meters) of his enclosure, then opened fire. The Indians did not expect the rapid firing of the new rifles and were thrown into confusion. However, only twenty-eight of Powell's men were left after this attack.

All day long (July 31, 1867), Chief Red Cloud, continued to push wave after wave of horsemen against Powell's position. Later, Red Cloud estimated that he had lost one thousand of his best braves. One old frontiersman with Powell had killed one hundred Indians. This humiliating defeat in the "Wagon Box" fight caused Red Cloud to lose face, and he never again took part in an important fight.

GLEAMING RAILS AND UPROARIOUS TOWNS

In 1867 General Grenville M. Dodge located a division point of the new transcontinental railroad and gave it the name of the Cheyenne Indians. J.R. Whitehead was the first settler in the new town of Cheyenne, and he sold railroad lots for one hundred fifty dollars. Some of the same lots brought a thousand dollars just a month later.

Congress had passed a bill providing for the Union Pacific railway system in 1862. One of the great problems was getting the railroad over the Continental Divide in Wyoming. However, General Dodge had discovered a pass over the Laramie Mountains, and he determined that this would be the location of the new railroad, over what is now called Sherman Hill. The government offered great subsidies for railroad building. The western part of the road was being built from California and the eastern part from Omaha. The more mileage each side could build, the more government money it could claim, and the great railroad building race was on.

The track crews laid rails so fast that supply towns had to be moved every few weeks. State historian Mrs. Cyrus Beard wrote, "Benton was undoubtedly the wickedest and most spectacular of the early settlements of Wyoming. The railroad was completed to that point in July, 1868, and it was a division station. A town of three thousand souls came into being as if by the wave of a wand . . . but the road was winning its way westward and in less than two months Benton had faded away."

But Cheyenne did not fade away. By November, 1867, when the railroad arrived there, the new city had grown to four thousand population—this in a period of only five months from its founding. A hundred fifty lots had brought twenty-five hundred dollars apiece. E.P. Snow and W.N. Monroe arrived in Cheyenne on August 15. Only forty-eight hours later they and local workmen had entirely completed a substantial building 55 feet (16.8 meters) long and 25 feet (7.6 meters) wide. This was typical of the city's mushroom growth. Its pleasant title was "Magic City of the Plains." When the railroad came, Cheyenne was known as "Hell on Wheels." The camp followers of the railroad were classed as "dregs of society." Cheyenne became probably "the greatest gambling center on the plains."

To add to the excitement, John Hardy and John Shaughnessy slugged it out in a prize fight of 126 rounds, and across the state gold was found near South Pass City.

By 1868, the transcontinental railroad had been practically finished across Wyoming. General Dodge wrote: "Every mile of road had to be surveyed, graded, tied and bridged under military protection. The order . . . was never to run when attacked. All were required to be armed and I do not know that the order was disobeyed . . . nor did I ever hear that the Indians had driven a party permanently from its work.... Each day taught us lessons by which we profited for the next, and our advance and improvements in the art of railroad construction were marked by the progress of the work, forty miles (64 kilometers) of track having been laid in 1865, two hundred and sixty (418 kilometers) in 1866, two hundred and forty (386 kilometers) in 1867, including the ascent to the summit of the Rock Mountains, at an elevation of 8,235 feet (2,510 meters)."

Building of this mighty railroad was one of the most remarkable accomplishments of mankind until that time. The effect the coming of the railroad had on Wyoming was almost incredible. Among the cities that sprang up practically overnight was Laramie. Only two weeks after the railroad entered, Laramie had grown to a town of five hundred buildings.

When the railroad was completed across the continent in 1869,

Cheyenne Frontier Days, a week-long celebration.

Across the
Continent, *by
Currier
and Ives.*

Wyoming was only a few days from either coast, where before it had been a tiresome, dangerous journey of weeks or months. A tremendous flow of the goods of all the world sped across the plains, where the herds of buffalo and the hostile Indians still wandered and sometimes interfered with the iron horses. Only a few years before, the almost empty spaces of Wyoming could be governed as part of the Dakota Territory from far away Yankton. Because of the railroad, the population of Wyoming had become larger than the other parts of Dakota Territory.

Now it was apparent that Wyoming must have a government of its own. On July 25, 1868, Congress created Wyoming Territory by the Organic Act of Wyoming, but the territorial government was not organized until May 19, 1869, with Cheyenne the capital. The name Wyoming was first used officially in that Organic Act. The first territorial governor was John A. Campbell, appointed by President U.S. Grant.

And so at last Wyoming had an identity of its own.

A modern cattle drive.

Yesterday and Today

It is an extraordinary tribute to the fairness and vision of the people of Wyoming that during its first year of organized government, the territory of Wyoming became "the first government in the world to give equal rights to women"—and this in a land where male residents were especially tough and "manly."

In 1870 at the district court in Laramie the first woman served on the jury, and this brought world attention to Wyoming. President Grant received a cable from King William of Prussia congratulating him for this example of "progress, enlightenment and civil liberty in America."

CONGRESS RECOGNIZES A WONDERLAND

In that year world attention also focused on Wyoming in another way. The first really scientific expedition reached Yellowstone. This was the Washburn-Langford-Doane party. One of the party wrote, "I think a more confirmed set of skeptics never went out into the wilderness than those who composed our party, and never was a party more completely surprised and captivated with the wonders of nature."

They first came to the Grand Canyon, then found mud springs, were the first to climb the lofty Absaroka Range, and marveled at the beauty of Yellowstone Lake. They marched for miles through pine forests and suddenly turned into a clearing to see with startled awe a giant column of water and steam shooting 150 feet (45.7 meters) into the air. After finding that this great geyser performed very regularly about every sixty minutes, the leader of the expedition, General Henry Washburn, named it Old Faithful.

The reports of the expedition caused a sensation. In one of the expedition's campfire conversations, Cornelius Hedges had said that such wonders ought to be held in trust by the government for use by all the people, and Mr. Hedges wrote an article for the Helena *Herald* of November 9, 1870, which is believed to be the first proposal of the national park idea. Bills were offered in Congress to create a national park at Yellowstone, and Dr. F.V. Hayden, of a later expedition, placed his wonderful photographs on display where they could be seen by all members of Congress.

Yellowstone became the first national park on March 1, 1872. Possibly no other act of Congress has been so widely approved. When the Earl of Dunraven visited the park in 1874 he wrote: "All honor then to the United States for having bequeathed as a free gift to man the beauties and curiosities of Wonderland. It was an act worthy of a great nation, and she will have her reward in the praise of the present army of tourists, no less than in the thanks of the generations of them yet to come."

LAST STAND

In 1874 General George A. Custer came into Wyoming with the largest and best-equipped force ever in the northwest until that time. He was to seek the best location for a proposed fort and also study the minerals of the region. At one time he camped in what he called Floral Valley. One of his party wrote: "The soldiers festooned their hats and their horses' bridles with flowers while the expedition's band, seated on an elevated rock ledge played ... 'The Mocking Bird,' 'The Blue Danube,' snatches from *Il Trovatore* and other popular tunes of the day. ... The music of the band was weird and fascinating." But this period of quiet life was not to last. The Indians had not yet entirely given up the idea that they could save their hunting grounds.

Only two years later, General Custer and his whole command were wiped out on the Little Bighorn River, not far north of the Wyoming border. After this battle two of the chiefs, Dull Knife and Little Wolf, brought their Cheyenne and Arapaho people to Red Canyon in Wyoming, where the Indians were routed by 1,100 soldiers under General Ranald Mackenzie.

From this time on, settlers and travelers in Wyoming were comparatively secure from Indian attack.

An Indian "incident" of a different kind in Wyoming was the flight of Chief Joseph and his whole Nez Percé group from eastern Washington and Oregon. Trying to get to safety in Canada, Chief Joseph led his people through the almost impossible travel of Yellowstone Park. This chief, who has been called "one of the greatest generals of his time," eluded three armies and safely made his way out of Yellowstone and Wyoming.

CATTLE COUNTRY

After the Civil War, there were millions of cattle in Texas that could be sold in the north and east if there were any way to get them there. Thousands were driven up the various trails to railroads or to ranches in the North. One of the most famous of these trails was the "Texas Trail" which crossed the eastern part of Wyoming from near Pine Bluffs and went as far as Miles City, Montana.

"One of the most unsual sights along the trail," according to Bill Bragg, Jr., "took place when a herd was sold to the government at an Indian agency. . . . The agent would call out a name: 'John Skinning Knife—two beeves!' The number of beeves would depend on the size of John's family. John, in all of his Indian finery, would mount his best hunting pony, and pull up alongside a chute while a steer was being driven into it. When the gate was thrown open he would drum his heels against the side of his horse, let out a war whoop, and draw up near the steer as fast as he could, letting drive with his arrows in the same manner he used when hunting buffalo in the pre-reservation days. As soon as he had dropped the animal, he would turn his pony back to the chute for a second steer while one or two—or even more of his squaws—would seek the fallen Texan longhorn and butcher it."

By 1884 it is estimated that more than 800,000 Texas cattle had been moved across Wyoming over the Texas Trail or the Long Trail.

In earlier days one of the California-bound wagon trains had been caught in a blizzard near the Laramie Plains. They had to turn their oxen loose and expected them to die in the winter. In the spring the oxen were found fat and sleek, and so it became clear that the Wyoming range was good for cattle. During 1870-80 cattlemen became "kings" in Wyoming. The lands were vast and unfenced. There was an unwritten law that mere "possession" controlled the land. Huge spring and fall roundups were held to brand the cattle and sort them for the markets. Horse raising was also very profitable.

One of the interesting developments in cattle ranching occurred when many foreign interests invested in ranching businesses. Many English gentlemen came to the Wyoming plains to establish cattle ranches. They built fashionable mansions in the nearest towns.

In 1883 Alexander H. Swan of England organized one of the greatest ranching corporations in the West—the Two Bar Cattle Company near Chugwater. At one time this huge operation had 120,000 head of cattle spread over 600,000 acres (242,810 hectares).

On one occasion, one hundred fifty of the English and Scottish owners of the Two Bar came to Wyoming to see their property. The first rodeo ever held in Wyoming was put on for these guests of the ranch. Bronc races, fancy pistol shooting, riding, roping, and an early version of rodeo clowns all entertained the visitors. One of them said it was the best show he had ever seen—worth coming 6,000 miles (9,656 kilometers).

By 1886, the tally of Wyoming stock had reached eight million head. Even towns were named for ranch brands, such as UVA and NODE. However, in the awful winter of 1887, cattle died by the thousands, and the "Cattle Barons" began to lose their hold on the country.

The first entry for a homestead in Wyoming was made in 1870. Soon more and more small ranchers and farmers began to come in and try to take over parts of the range or even to homestead on land claimed by ranchers. There was a constant feud between these "nesters" and the larger ranchers. Also involved were the many rustlers. In 1892 a strange incident of our history occurred. Later this came to be known as the Johnson County Cattle War, fought by the ranchers on one side and the nesters and rustlers on the other.

This came about when Johnson County nesters and small ranchers decided to have an early roundup. This would have made it easier for rustlers to round up mavericks and otherwise get the upper hand of big ranchers. The big ranchers organized a group called the Regulators. They hired gunmen from many states and placed them under the command of a former army officer. They marched on the K.C. Ranch and killed two men. The leading merchant of Buffalo, Robert Foote, became the "Paul Revere" of this "war" by galloping over the area on his black horse, with his black cape and long white beard flowing in the wind, warning everyone of the attack. He then opened his store and gave free guns and ammunition to the defenders. The sheriff swore in one hundred deputies, and several hundred others were organized to defend the town.

The defenders cornered the Regulators at the T.A. Ranch south of Buffalo. They were about to storm the ranch when army troops arrived, and the Regulators were saved by the cavalry. The army had to be kept in Buffalo some time until the excitement passed.

Branding cattle.

TAMING THE "WILD WEST"

In new country, orderly government takes some time to develop. Meanwhile, some of the worst characters are attracted by the lack of lawful procedures. This was true for a time in many areas of Wyoming, where events have provided stories for many a scene in television and movie "westerns."

Almost from its beginning Laramie was terrorized by desperadoes. By autumn of 1868 there were enough law abiding citizens to take action, and almost five hundred of them descended on the haunts of the outlaws. Most of the town took part in the gun battle that followed. Five men were killed; four outlaws were hanged from telegraph poles. Unfortunately, the outlaws soon infiltrated the vigilantes and eventually controlled the legal government. Affairs became so bad that the federal courts had to take over for a time until Wyoming territory could get control. In 1876 Jack McCall was arrested in Laramie for shooting Wild Bill Hickok in the head at Deadwood, South Dakota.

When the one-room jail at Cheyenne was full, a mob would take the petty offenders to the edge of town and ask them which way they wanted to go. They were turned in the proper direction and told to "Git!" If they failed to hurry fast enough, they would hear the thud of bullets from six shooters as they hit the dirt back of their heels. A local newspaper says that the vigilante committee at Cheyenne was "characterized more by restraint than by excess of zeal."

At Rawlins in 1878 vigilantes hanged one outlaw, and twenty-four others were warned that the same thing would happen to them. At the Rawlins railroad station the next morning, exactly twenty-four tickets were sold for out of town destinations.

A notorious hideout for outlaws was a valley known as "the Hole in the Wall" near Kaycee. From this sanctuary, the bandits would sweep out to raid and annoy communities over a vast area. As late as 1894, Hole in the Wall outlaws took possession of Thermopolis during an election. By evening they were driven out by citizens in a battle led by Judge Joe Magill, "with knee leggings, .45 Colts, and full cartridge belts . . . the air of a commanding general."

Not all the "wild west" stories of Wyoming are so grim. A well-known reporter, Olga Moore, wrote in the Sheridan *Post-Enterprise* an amusing account of one event: "One Mr. Morris, a gentleman of energy and temper, became excited during the course of festivities and beat up several of the prominent citizens of the town. Marshal Reed made the arrest with promptness, but he had no court to try him and no place to put him. . . . He finally incarcerated the prisoner in the livery stable, but the belligerent Mr. Morris escaped.

"However, the arm of the law was long. . . . Nearly a year later Mr. Reed ran across Mr. Morris . . . and informed him that he was still under arrest. The jail breaker amiably accompanied him back to town. The spring floods were raging and the Goose Creeks were roaring torrents impossible to cross. The Justice of the Peace, George Brundage, lived across the river and was cut off from his civic duties. Marshal Reed and his prisoner created such an uproar that Mr. Brundage rushed out to see the excitement.

"By dint of much shouting Reed conveyed to him the glad tidings that their first prisoner was once more under arrest and that Sheridan's first trial was about to begin. The Justice of the Peace lifted his voice above the thunder of the flood and sent back the memorable verdict: 'Fine him $10 and costs!' "

A MORE SETTLED STATE

The great period of Wyoming settlement did not come until the 1880s. Often only the bare necessities were available. Even white bread and potatoes were luxuries. Everthing was used in some way. For example, a good lamp could be made from a syrup can and candle. However, to give interest to life, there were literary societies and the Sunday schools and much informal debating about the news of the world. In spite of the hardships, according to Oliver Hanna, "the early days of the pioneer were the happy days."

In 1890 Wyoming's population was only 62,500—not enough to qualify as a state. In spite of this fact, Congress passed the necesssary legislation and on July 10 of that year Wyoming was admitted as the

Pioneer's Home, *by Currier and Ives.*

forty-fourth state, with the last territorial governor, Francis E. Warren, as new state governor.

A great celebration took place in Cheyenne. The *Anvil Chorus* was
sung with an accompaniment of real anvils. Artillery fired forty-four
guns. There was to have been a balloon ascension, but it failed.
Almost everyone in town took part in the giant parade. All the
merchants were on hand for the parade, including "Mrs. Robinson,
in a jaunty rig, who showed what she is doing in the ice cream, fruit
and vegetable line. She had a fat boy, dressed up gaily, with a placard
on the wagon saying: 'I eat Mrs. Robinson's ice cream.'"

In addition to statehood, another significant event took place in
1890—Fort Laramie was closed by the army, and sixty-five of its
buildings were auctioned off to homesteaders for use as lumber. The
frontier had gone, and there was no longer any need for soldiers in
one of the most historic strongholds in all of the West.

Frontiersman William "Buffalo Bill" Cody founded the town of Cody in 1897. Wyoming was the first state to fill its quota of volunteers for the Spanish-American War in 1898. In fact, the state achieved four and a half times its quota of volunteers. That year also saw the Grand Teton conquered by the first climber.

In 1902 Yellowstone Forest Reserve was created, and this was the beginning of what has since become our mammoth system of national forests. To protect this forest, the first ranger station was established in 1903-1904 on the Cody Road.

The peak of the difficulty between cattlemen and sheepmen occurred in the early 1900s. Sheep were introduced into Wyoming in 1878. Early cattle ranchers hated sheep because they cropped the range grass too close, and because they said cattle would not graze where sheep had been. Also, they thought the range was already too crowded. Cattlemen who raided sheep ranches were known as "gunnysackers" because of the sack disguise they wore over their heads.

They "marked off deadlines on the range, burned some sheep wagons, shot at and mistreated some of the herders." Some herds were dynamited, others "rimrocked"—that is, driven over the rims of cliffs—or dogs were turned loose on the sheep. However, as one account says, "It soon became apparent that the most bitter 'gunnysackers' entered the sheep business with resulting prosperity to themselves and firm establishment of the industry in the country. . . ."

In 1906 explorer-President Theodore Roosevelt visited Yellowstone Park on a camping trip, and in that same year he created the country's first national monument—Wyoming's Devils Tower.

Wyoming had cause for its celebration of the first great continental highway across the United States. When the Lincoln Highway was opened in 1913, 450 miles (724 kilometers) of Wyoming roadway had become part of the "Main Street" of the United States. On the night of the celebration, a string of bonfires glittered along the highway clear across the state.

Also in 1913, Buffalo Bill held his last big-game hunt at Camp Monaco in Wyoming. The camp took its name from Prince Albert of Monaco, who was there with many other world celebrities.

From such festivities Wyoming soon turned to the grim realities of World War I. Seven percent of the entire population of Wyoming served in this conflict—a total of 11,393. The sturdy character of Wyoming people is shown by the fact that among those drafted in the state, Wyoming had the highest percentage of men accepted of all the states.

During the administration of President Warren Harding, leases were made with private companies for the valuable oil properties in the Wyoming Teapot Dome area. Later it was discovered that fraud and irregularities had occurred. For their part in this, oil tycoon Harry F. Sinclair, of the Sinclair Oil Company, received a six-and-a-half-month jail sentence, and the United States Secretary of the Interior Albert B. Fall was given a year in prison, plus a one hundred thousand dollar fine. This so-called "Teapot Dome Scandal" remains even today as the principal memory of the Harding administration. Senator John B. Kendrick of Wyoming was one of the investigators of the scandal.

On the same day in 1924 two states elected women to be their governors. One of these states was Texas, the other Wyoming, with its Governor-elect Nellie Tayloe Ross whose election helped to carry out the pioneer Wyoming tradition of recognizing the rights and abilities of women.

Grand Teton National Park was created in 1929. In 1938 the United States government granted the Shoshone Indians four million dollars for their lands within the Wind River Reservation, which they had permitted the Arapaho to use ever since the great reservation had been created.

A strange episode occurred in 1939 when some residents of Sheridan and other northern areas became dissatisfied with the state government and "seceded" to form the state of Absaroka. They said this new "state" contained most of the land north of the North Platte River, including Yellowstone Park. Of course, this "49th state" never really came close to existing.

The federal government helped Wyoming celebrate its fiftieth anniversary as a state, in 1940, by issuing a handsome anniversary stamp.

The Teton Mountain Range.

Wyoming contributed to the mighty American effort of World War II in many ways, principally through the service of thousands of her sons and daughters, many of whom died in the conflict.

Another natural area of nationwide importance came under federal protection when Jackson Hole was made a national monument in 1950. Ten years later one of the truly historic localities in the country became Fort Laramie National Historic Site.

In 1965, statewide celebrations recognized the seventy-fifth anniversary of Wyoming's statehood. The whole history of statehood could easily have passed during one lifetime. In that lifetime, the state had gone from the bow and arrow to the intercontinental rocket—from Conestoga wagon and stagecoach to supersonic planes and men in orbital flights around the earth—from crude frontiersmen to the most advanced scientists.

And yet the lure of the plains remains; the wonders of geyser and waterfall and calm of lofty mountains continue to offer their comfort and pleasure to mankind.

51

Right: A prairie dog. Below: Prairie Dog Town, *by George Catlin.*

Natural Treasures

ANIMALS: ONE APIECE

The plains are "peopled with large villages of what are called prairie dogs, because they utter a short sharp bark..." The writer was English traveler Isabella Bird, telling about her trip on the train from Cheyenne. "We passed numbers of their villages.... On nearly every rim a small furry reddish-buff beast sat on his hind legs.... These creatures were acting as sentinels and sunning themselves. As we passed, each gave a warning yelp, shook its tail, and, with a ludicrous flourish of its hind legs dived into its hole.... From its enormous increase and the energy and extent of its burrowing operations one can fancy that in the course of years the prairies will be seriously injured, as it honeycombs the ground."

Writer Bird's prediction was far from true. Today the prairie dog is just one of the vanishing creatures that used to spread over the plains in countless numbers. As early as 1941 a prairie dog town in Devils Tower National Monument was placed under protection of the Park Service in order to help preserve at least one of these villages.

The pastures of Wyoming were so perfect for stock that innumerable buffalo once flourished there. Even as recently as the time of the railroad, trains were sometimes delayed for hours as buffalo passed in herds stretching from horizon to horizon. Buffalo were so thick that a six-pound cannon fired at Fort Laramie killed thirty with one shot. The buffalo considered telegraph poles to be their personal scratching posts, and a number of buffalo could shove a pole out of the ground in a short time. As protection, the linemen stuck pointed spokes into the poles. These made the poles so much better for scratching that at every pole between Cheyenne and Omaha lines of twenty-five or thirty buffalo had formed, waiting their turns to get at the wonderful scratching places.

The enormous herds of buffalo are gone, wiped out by man. Only a few herds are protected and are thriving in such places as Yellowstone Park.

Most of the large animals of Wyoming are not now decreasing in numbers. Yellowstone is one of the greatest wild animal sanctuaries in the world. The 23,500-acre (9,510-hectare) Jackson Hole National Elk Refuge preserves the world's largest herd of elk (or wapiti)—numbering almost ten thousand head. It is estimated that there is at least one big game animal for every man, woman, and child resident of Wyoming, including the mighty moose, pronghorn (or American) antelope, mule deer, grizzly and black bear, mountain lion (gradually disappearing), bobcats, Canada lynx, wolverine, and the fantastic Rocky Mountain sheep, now mostly in the Gros Ventre Mountains. Wyoming is known as one of the world's foremost hunting grounds.

Smaller animals include golden manteled marmot, white-tailed jackrabbits, ground squirrels, pocket gophers, northern plains skunk, beaver, mink, marten, badger, coyote, fox, weasel, shrew, and Rocky Mountain jumping mice.

One of Wyoming's best-known animals was an evil white luster wolf who killed twenty-five thousand dollars worth of livestock before it was killed.

Writer Grant Jones made a reputation by creating imaginary creatures of Wyoming, such as the six-legged Cogly Woo. When chased, the Cogly Woo, he said, bored a hole in the ground with its tail, jumped into the hole and pulled the hole after him. The imaginary Backaboar was adapted to mountain life by having shorter legs on one side than the other. He could be captured by turning him around so that his shorter legs were on the downhill side, according to Jones.

In winter large herds of elk migrate to graze in the National Elk Refuge near Jackson.

54

FLYING AND SWIMMING

Among the great birds of Wyoming are the fabulous trumpeter swan, the bald eagle, the great Canada goose, wild turkey, the osprey, and pelicans of Molly Island in Yellowstone Lake. Pelican wingspreads sometimes reach 9 feet (2.7 meters). The most widely distributed game bird is the sage grouse. Sage cocks still perform their eccentric dance not far from city centers.

The sprightly water ouzel often has its nest behind a waterfall and dashes underwater along the bottoms of swift mountain streams searching for food. Other Wyoming birds include mountain chickadee, bittern, junco (twenty varieties), cinnamon teal, grackle, lark bunting, Macgillivray warbler, willow-thrush, plumbeous vireo, mountain song sparrow, western tanager, towhee, McGown longspur, Lewis woodpecker, sharp-shinned hawk, Wright flycatcher, long-tailed chat, and western mockingbird.

Other varieties include red-breasted sapsucker, crested bufflehead, broad-tail hummingbird, barrow golden eye, Audubon hermit thrush, three-toed woodpecker, Rocky Mountain creeper, carmine grosbeak, rosy finch, titlark, crowned kinglet, and pipit.

Eighty-three species of native fish have been found in Wyoming waters. About twenty of these are game fish. Of these, the cutthroat is the only native trout. Not a game fish, but especially popular for ice fishing, is the ling fish. This is a variety of whitefish that sometimes grows 4 feet (1.2 meters) long and is said to taste like trout.

GROWING THINGS

Those who think of Wyoming as an arid land will be astounded at the enormous variety of plant life. There are 2,500 kinds of seed-bearing plants and as many ferns, mosses, and algae. Yellowstone Park alone has 750 varieties of wild flowers. The vast Wyoming grazing lands were carpeted with 150 different kinds of grass.

In the drier areas are greasewood, a quick burning fuel, and sage, both black and silver. Sage is actually a small tree, thickly branched.

Settlers drove most of the mountain lions out of Wyoming.

The mountain meadows and slopes are covered with an unbelievable variety of flowers. In the highlands such as the Snowy Range, these are often dwarfed varieties, including orchids, buttercups, snowdrops—all in tiny miniatures.

Wild rose, thimbleberry, daisy, purple aster, fireweed, Indian paintbrush (the state flower), and Rose of Sharon spread their color over the Tetons.

Other Wyoming flowers of many regions include shooting star, cowslip, columbine, forget-me-not, Jacob's ladder, saxifrage, miner's candle, drabas, windflower, fire weed, evening star, kinnikinnic, five fingers, rabbit brush, globeflower, elephant head, yellow water lily, soapweed yucca, sunflower, prickly pear cactus, balsam root, twinflower, fritillary, and sedum.

Almost 3,500,000 acres (1,416,400 hectares) of Wyoming are covered with commercial forests, which would provide twelve billion board feet of live saw timber. Most popular commercial timber are lodgepole pine, Engelman spruce, Douglas fir, white fir, and ponderosa pine. Other needle trees include yellow and whitebark pine, blue and white spruce, Rocky Mountain cedar, Utah juniper, and Alpine fir.

Much of the commercial timberland is protected in national forests, and the national forest idea originated in Wyoming, with the first federal timber preserve in the United States.

Quaking aspen is the most common broad-leaved tree in Wyoming. Its autumn colors of gold and orange are brilliant on the slopes. The course of rivers and streams sometimes can be traced for miles following the pattern of the willows that grow along their banks. Poplar, birch, alder, hawthorne, mountain mahogany, and serviceberry are all Wyoming trees. The giant blue oak is said to be the only oak that is native to Wyoming. After the disastrous dust storms of the thirties, shelter belts of Chinese elm, pine, and Russian olive were very successfully planted to keep the soil from blowing away.

MINERAL WEALTH

Wyoming is a great storehouse of mineral wealth ready for industrial development. There are seventy known mineral classifications in the state, including aggregates, anorthosite, bentonite, copper, glass sand, gypsum, iron, phosphate, sodium, sulphur, titanium, trona, uranium, thorium, and rare earths. Mineral fuels and coal are among the most important.

The petroleum reserves in Wyoming rank sixth among all the states. It is said that coal underlies 41 percent of the entire state, and as early as 1941 it was estimated that Wyoming possessed the largest coal reserves in the United States.

Almost every community has its Rock Hound clubs, made of eager searchers for rare and beautiful rocks and gems. In Wyoming an extraordinary variety of these can be found, including alabaster, onyx, marble, agate, petrified wood, quartz, jade, chalcedony, garnet, rhodonite, sapphire, gastrolith, azurite, malachite, bloodstone, and ruby. One of the most popular pastimes for visitors is searching for prize rock and gem finds.

WATER OF LIFE

No natural resource is more vital than water. Contrary to what most people would believe, Wyoming water is abudant. It is estimated that there is enough water in Wyoming for the industrial, agricultural, and personal needs of several million more people than today live in the state.

The great quantities of ground water are little used because surface waters can be diverted so easily. The Natural Resources Board includes the protection of water supplies among its many other duties.

57

Charcoal kilns at Piedmont.

58

The People Use Their Treasures

The Eaton brothers originally operated a ranch in North Dakota. However, they had so many friends who liked to spend time on their ranch that finally the friends began to insist on paying so that the Eatons would not lose money by their hospitality.

When they moved to their new ranch on Wolf Creek near Dayton, the Eatons began to develop a complete program for paying guests, and from this beginning grew the great dude ranch industry of today.

However, livestock still continues as the largest part of Wyoming's agricultural activities. Eighty percent of the state's agricultural income is received from livestock. The Wyoming Stock Growers Association was organized in 1873, and it has included a large percentage of the influential and wealthy men of the state. Cattle and calves make up three-fourths of the Wyoming livestock industry.

Thousands of Wyoming's horses were sold for service in World War I. Most of the state's horses now are the cow ponies, said to be as skillful as their masters in all the intricate arts of working the range. Dairying is also a fast-growing industry.

Wyoming is second in the nation in sheep and wool production and first in average fleece weights. Sheep flourished in Wyoming on vast acreages where no other animal could find a living.

Mormon colonists experimented with irrigation as early as 1853, and irrigated acreage is continuing to grow. Dry farming, begun in 1878 by Swedish settlers, has had successes and failures causing much farm poverty. Great damage was done by erosion in dry farming areas, and intensive efforts have restored many of these areas.

Hay is Wyoming's number one crop. Two thirds of the state's harvested acreage is in hay. Leading cash crops are wheat, sugar beets, and dry beans.

MINERALS

Oil is the leading industry in Wyoming's economy today, with 9,500 producing wells in the state. It ranks fifth among all the states in oil production. Commercial quantities of oil were discovered in Wyoming as early as 1888. The first oil well was drilled at Lander. Oil at Casper came in in 1890, and by 1895 there was a small refinery there. Casper's largest oil boom, in the Salt Creek Oil Field, began in 1915, and this was considered one of the world's greatest light oil fields. Natural gas comes from 107 Wyoming fields at the rate of more than 350 billion cubic feet (about 10 billion cubic meters) per year.

When the railroads arrived, mining of Wyoming's great coal supplies quickly got under way. Many Polish families settled near Sheridan to work the coal mines there. With the changeover of railroads from coal to oil, coal mining declined in the state, especially around the Rock Springs area.

Gold was discovered in the South Pass district of Wind River Mountains as early as 1842. Carissa lode was discovered at South Pass in 1867. Recently South Pass has again become important in mining. Iron is now mined in the region, and Geneva Steel has a big processing plant there. Lander's gold rush began in 1868. Seven Swedish miners took seven thousand dollars worth of gold from their mine near Buffalo in just three days. However, the location of the mine became lost, and this is just one of the many "lost" mines of Wyoming, for which people still vainly search.

The Indians had mined iron ore at Sunrise in prehistoric times, probably for body coloring pigments. Iron ore is the only metallic mineral presently being worked in Wyoming, although it is hoped that copper mining may again become practical. There was a copper mining boom at Encampment in the early 1900s but the bubble soon burst.

The Indians also long used the salt fields near Auburn. These are said to be 99.99 percent pure salt. The pioneer salt fields near Newcastle were invaluable in providing this essential mineral during early days.

Rawlins has an unsual distinction in the mineral field. It has given its name to a color—Rawlins red. The paint pigment mines there sent the Rawlins red used to paint the Brooklyn Bridge in New York when it was first built.

Riverton has been called the "Mining Capital of Wyoming," with five ore processing mills located there.

Limestone, cement rock, gypsum, and pumice are at the top in the nonmetallic mineral production of Wyoming.

More than 1,500,000 short tons (1,361,000 metric tons) of uranium are produced in the state each year, making uranium the third mineral in value in Wyoming production. In 1962 a ten million dollar trona mine and soda ash refining plant was opened near Green River, to produce up to 600,000 tons (544,300 metric tons) of soda ash per year. The trona reserves are estimated at 200 million tons (181 million metric tons).

TRANSPORTATION AND COMMUNICATION

As early as 1851 a semi-monthly stagecoach service had been established across Wyoming over the old Oregon Trail. In that same year the first and only steamboat in the state's history struggled up the North Platte as far as the present-day site of Guernsey Dam. By 1858 daily passenger and mail stages were crossing Wyoming. Rock Springs became an important repair point on the stage lines. After 1862 the southern or "Overland" route was used instead of the Oregon Trail. The State Historical Society and a number of the county historical societies have organized summer treks over some of the old trails. Over a period of several years, the old Oregon Trail has been retraced and parts of the Morman Trail have also been followed.

Even after the transcontinental railroad placed Wyoming on the mainline of cross-country travel, stages continued to be important. From 1876 to 1887 the Cheyenne to Black Hills stage line carried important and unusual passengers and cargo, including a ton (.9 metric ton) of gold from Deadwood, South Dakota, protected by eleven horsemen with Winchester rifles ready.

Another cargo was Phatty Thompson's cats. Thompson had a market for cats in Deadwood. He paid the children of Cheyenne twenty-five cents each for cats and soon collected a huge crateful which he put on the stage for Deadwood. When the stage tipped over on the route, the cats were scattered in every direction, but they finally came back, and Phatty collected from ten to twenty-five dollars each for his cats.

As the years went by, the stage routes were converted to modern highways; the daring Pony Express riders were replaced by telegraph, telephone, radio, television, and air mail, as Wyoming and the nation grew up.

Wyoming's first newpaper was the Fort Bridger *Daily Telegraph,* begun in 1863, but it is not now being published. The Cheyenne *Leader,* founded 1867, now part of the Wyoming *State Tribune,* is the oldest continuing paper in the state.

OTHER ACTIVITIES

As early as 1864, charcoal kilns of Wyoming were providing fuel for pioneer smelters. By 1870 Wyoming had thirty-four manufacturing establishments with a capital investment of one million dollars. Today, the primary industries depend on the mineral, timber, livestock, and agricultural resources of the state. Cheese, flour, beet-sugar manufacture, and printing are important. Forest products account for 12 percent of the state's manufacturing payroll. The petroleum and coal industries are the largest employers of the state. Such products as beautiful hand-tooled leather saddles continue to add a picturesque quality to Wyoming's many products.

Human Treasures

MASTERS OF THE FRONTIER

Jim Bridger was one of the most picturesque people in early Wyoming. At the age of eighteen he came to Wyoming to assist General William H. Ashley. For fifty years, Bridger led tough frontiersmen "like children." One of his friends, Samuel Stringer, said of Bridger, "His wonderful ability as a guide must have been a gift, as others whose experience had been as great failed to reach the high standard of efficiency which so characterized his work as a scout. . . . He was a wonderful man and those who followed his advice usually came out all right. While he had no knowledge of engineering, his ability to map out any part of the territory entirely from memory was uncanny. He knew the Indians and their habits."

A famous western doctor, Marcus Whitman, met Bridger at the fur rendezvous in 1835 and removed a 3-inch (76.2-millimeter) arrowhead which had been imbedded in Bridger's shoulder for a year. He had been hit by a Blackfoot Indian.

Bridger was one of the nation's greatest storytellers. A favorite story was about the petrified forest, where he tried to jump across a gorge. He did not jump far enough and would have fallen, but the air, he said, was also petrified and held him up. In this forest he said he saw "Peetrified birds singing on peetrified trees." In order to find the elevation of a place, he said he simply bored a hole till he found salt water and measured the depth of the hole.

Bridger was thoroughly familiar with Yellowstone. But because of his many tall tales almost no one believed his Yellowstone stories. His most celebrated Yellowstone story concerned the obsidian (or glass) cliff, which he truly first discovered. However, he had to dress up the story. He said he shot at an elk but the animal refused to fall. He took several more shots and then went up to knock it over, but ran into a mountain of glass that protected the animal from being shot. In fact, he said, the mountain acted like a magnifying glass, and the elk was actually more than 20 miles (32 kilometers) away.

John Colter's career was also a most unusual one. He had been a valued member of the Lewis and Clark expedition. He left the expedition to trap in the Yellowstone River Company, where he finally took up with the fur company of Manuel Lisa.

His accomplishments loom large; he was first to discover the source of the Snake River, first to explore the Bighorn and Wind rivers, first to see what is now Wyoming, first to see the Tetons, Jackson Hole, and, most of all, first to discover Yellowstone Park.

When he returned to "civilization" in St. Louis, where he married, his stories were laughed at, and he became the subject of ridicule. In 1813 he died of jaundice as an unknown to fame. He was buried in a graveyard on what is now called Tunnel Hill, near Dundee, Missouri. The railroad, unaware of the forgotten graves, dug up the hill, so that even John Colter's grave has been lost in the passage of years. He remains one of America's neglected heroes, with his only monument the tracks of the Missouri Pacific Railroad.

International renown came to a frontiersman of more recent date—William "Buffalo Bill" Cody. In Wyoming, as a fifteen-year-old boy, Cody made the longest ride in the history of the Pony Express, 322 miles (518.2 kilometers). He had to keep on going when he found that his replacement had been killed.

One young Wyoming pioneer told of seeing Buffalo Bill and Wild Bill Hickok playing cards in a saloon in 1867. Each one wore a handsome jacket of buckskin and had long hair, to their shoulders. The boy wrote, "I swore there and then that some day I'd own a jacket like theirs, but I was not so enthusiastic about the long hair."

Much of Buffalo Bill's later life centered in Wyoming. He founded the town of Cody, built the Irma Hotel, named for his daughter, and led many hunting expeditions in the region.

INDIAN CHIEFS

Few of the world's leaders have ruled so long or in such an unusual manner as Wyoming's great Shoshone chief—Washakie. It has been said of him that he "understood the history of his time bet-

A striking statue of Buffalo Bill dominates Cody, the community named in his honor.

ter than many statesmen." For sixty years he held sway as the benevolent dictator of his people. He was able to comprehend in a way few other Indian leaders could that the Europeans were too many and too strong to be kept from the Indian lands forever. He never fought the Europeans, but co-operated with them so skillfully that he brought brilliant results for the welfare of his people.

Many reminders of the great chief remain today in Wyoming, including the town of Fort Washakie. He was buried near the town after living more than a hundred years, according to some accounts.

Two Indian leaders who were among the most violent in opposing the settlers were Red Cloud and his son-in-law, Crazy Horse.

When the government abandoned the Powder River Country, Red Cloud thought he had won. However, he soon saw this was only a temporary gain and eventually was forced to settle on a reservation, after taking one last battle fling at his old enemies the Shoshone. In later years, he went to Washington, D.C., on several occasions and died in 1909.

NOTABLE WOMEN

Because of Wyoming's pioneer interest in protecting women's rights, it is not surprising that Wyoming women have been among the earliest to gain reputations in public affairs. One of those most responsible for the territory's decision to give equal rights for women was Esther Hobart Morris. In 1870 she became the first woman jurist, in the position of Justice of the Peace at South Pass. She became known as "The Mother of Woman Suffrage."

After serving as one of the two first women governors of a state, Nellie Tayloe Ross became one of the first women to serve in high positions in the national government. President Franklin Delano Roosevelt appointed her as director of the Mint in 1933, and she served in this post for twenty years until 1953, when she resigned.

One of the most famous scouts of the plains was not a man but a woman—Martha Canary. She was better known by another name, and she herself told how that name came to her: "It was on Goose Creek, Wyoming, where the town of Sheridan is now. Captain Egan was in command.... We were ordered out to quell an uprising of the Indians.... Returning to the post we were ambushed.... Captain Egan was shot. I ... saw the captain reeling in his saddle as though about to fall. I turned my horse and galloped back ... and got there in time to catch him as he was falling. I lifted him onto my horse in front of me and succeeded in getting him safely to the post. Captain, on recovering, laughingly said, 'I name you Calamity Jane, the heroine of the plains.' "

CREATIVE PEOPLE

Wyoming's best-known writer is probably Owen Wister, who wrote his popular *The Virginian* in 1902. This book assured the cowboy a place in American fiction.

One of the most popular novels about Wyoming was *The Covered Wagon* by Emerson Hough. It gave everlasting glamour to the old Oregon Trail and the clumsy vehicles that moved over it.

Another "trail" was turned into successful fiction by that most famous of all Western writers—Zane Grey. He stayed in Wyoming long enough to gather material for his book *U.P. Trail.*

A working rancher, John Olay, who managed Wyoming's largest cattle outfit, also became a successful author with his book *My Life on the Range.* Struthers Burt, a professor, novelist, and poet, transplanted to Wyoming from the East, wrote *Powder River,* called by some the best book ever written about Wyoming. Mrs. Burt also became a popular writer.

One of the country's leading humorists was Edgar Watson "Bill" Nye, who gained his first fame in writing about Wyoming, where he was a lawyer, postmaster, and editor at Laramie.

Among Wyoming's better-known artists are Hans Kleiber and Thomas Moran. Kleiber was a forest ranger, who taught himself the skills necessary to do prize-winning etchings. He is also known for his work in water colors. Moran was born in England but did much of his best work in Wyoming. His great panorama painting called *The Grand Canyon of the Yellowstone* was bought by the government for ten thousand dollars for the Capitol galleries in Washington. Mount Moran in the Tetons was named in his honor. He was often accompanied by his friend the pioneer western photographer, William H. Jackson—one of the most notable photographic artists America has produced.

E.W. Gollings, known as the "Cowboy Artist," was famous around the world for his paintings of the West. Several of his paintings hang in the capitol at Cheyenne. The American artist who was a main figure in the abstract impressionist movement, Jackson Pollock, was born in Cody.

SUCH INTERESTING PEOPLE

Department store tycoon J.C. Penney, who created a merchandising empire of hundreds of stores during his long lifetime, opened his first store at Kemmerer.

Among notable public figures of Wyoming was John B. Kendrick.

*J.C. Penney, the
department store tycoon.*

He began his career as a rancher, becoming an authority on livestock, cattle diseases, and marketing, and president of the Wyoming Stockgrowers Association. He served as governor of Wyoming and United States Senator from 1916 until his death in 1933. William H. Bright was nationally known as a champion of the rights of women, and it was the bill he introduced which gave women full franchise in Wyoming, at such an early date. The well-known mayor of Chicago, "Big Bill" Thompson, got his start as a cow puncher at Moorcroft.

Almost a legend among the old-timers was Jacques La Ramie, a trapper along the North Platte, whose name has been given to a city, a fort, a mountain range, a mountain, a county, a river, and a section of the plains. Another early settler was Jim Baker, who adopted such Indian customs as having his two wives attend to his trapping lines. One of his greatest pleasures was said to have been sitting in the clearing before his headquarters near Savery while his wives groomed his long glowing hair and beard.

Tim McCoy began his life as an opera singer, but his voice failed, and he drifted west to live on the Shoshone reservation. Later he became adjutant general of Wyoming, then opened a dude ranch and gained great popular success in becoming one of the most noted early stars of western motion pictures.

Among early religious leaders no name is better known than that of Father Pierre J. De Smet, who was born in Belgium in 1801, but who became one of the greatest authorities on the American West as well as one of the most beloved men in the country. Among his notable achievements was celebration of the first Catholic mass in Wyoming—at Pinedale.

The Indians of Wyoming expected miracles of their priests or medicine men. Before they would accept Father De Smet, they wanted him to show his power. A chief requested him to place his hand on the head of an enraged buffalo bull. The priest did this, expecting to be tossed high on the animal's horns. However, his silver crucifix glittered in the sun, and the animal seemed hypnotized. Father De Smet scratched the animal behind the ear, to the delight of the Indians, who thought this was powerful "medicine."

The Reverend John Roberts founded the Shoshone mission boarding school and carried on a remarkable work among the Indians for forty years. He translated portions of the Bible into the Shoshone and Arapaho languages.

Old Main, the first building on the University of Wyoming campus.

Teaching and Learning

On September 6, 1887, the "nation's highest university," the University of Wyoming at Laramie, opened its doors for the first time. Wyoming was one of the few states to have a public university before reaching statehood. On the first faculty was Professor Avon Nelson, who soon gained wide attention for the university by his outstanding work in botany. He began the university's unique Rocky Mountain Herbarium, now with more than 150,000 species of plants and animals. Later, Professor Nelson became president of the university.

Another outstanding university collection is that of the Geologic Museum. The university maintains a summer science study camp in the Snowy Range Nature Area and operates a notable experimental farm to improve Wyoming dairy cattle, livestock, grains, hays, and vegetables and find the most suitable strains and procedures for the Western region.

When Dr. A.G. Crane came to be president of the university in 1923, he received a "typical" Wyoming welcome. Masked riders stopped his car at gunpoint, and placed him and his family in an old Concord coach. With five hundred students mounted on cow ponies, whooping and shooting, the procession moved to the fairgrounds at Laramie, where Dr. Crane was crowned "King of the Cowboys."

The university is noted for its "Lore" degrees. Summer students are encouraged to learn more about the outdoors by trying to qualify for nonacademic "degrees" in riding, roping, mountain climbing, catching fish, and identifying animals and plants. The degrees are awarded at a great barbecue of wild game, including bear and various members of the deer family.

The notable appearance of university buildings is due to the fact that the institution owns its own quarries of an unusual and attractive pink sandstone.

Other educational institutions are Eastern Wyoming College, Torrington; Central Wyoming College, Riverton; and Western Community College at Rock Springs.

The first school in Wyoming was opened by the Rev. William

Still standing is Wyoming's first school building,
which has been restored at Fort Bridger State Historic Site.

Vaux at Fort Laramie in 1852. The first schoolhouse at Fort Bridger opened in 1860. Cheyenne dedicated its first school with the spectators shivering in -23 degrees Fahrenheit (-30.6 degrees Celsius) weather. The people of Shell Creek were so eager for a school that they opened one in a stable, with the children sitting in the manger. A pair of black rubber boots, split down the middle, served as a blackboard.

One reason for the outstanding quality of Wyoming's public schools today is the support received from the 3,000,000 acres (1,214,100 hectares) of state oil lands set apart to finance the schools.

Enchantment of Wyoming

WHERE NATURE COMES TO A BOIL

In 1935 an old Bannock Indian named Whitehawk was being shown through Yellowstone Park. When asked what he thought about all these wonders, he replied that he thought it was a good place to cook. Others with greater powers of description have said that nowhere in the world is the visitor struck with such a sense of nature's power and mystery.

Here the great forces below the earth, which are generally bottled up, come to the surface for all to see. There are three thousand hot springs and geysers. A geyser is formed when cold waters are able to trickle down into the ground and strike superheated volcanic rock far below. They boil and surge into steam. If this takes place in a tube formation of rock hard enought to stand the pressures, the super-heated water and steam are forced up out of the ground with tremendous pressure and hurled into the air.

The most famous of all geysers, of course, is Old Faithful. It is not the largest, but it is the most regular, and one of the most beautiful, shooting 115 to 150 feet (35 to 45.7 meters) into the air about every 65 minutes. It is not considered very old, possibly only four or five hundred years.

Giant Geyser is the largest of the Yellowstone geysers now flowing, reaching 250 feet (76 meters) with an enormous flow of water. However, conditions in Yellowstone are constantly changing. On the fiftieth anniversary of the park, a new geyser suddenly erupted to a height of 300 feet (91.4 meters) and was named Semi-Centennial Geyser. It is not now active. The Hayden expedition in 1870 counted 680 active geysers in Lower Basin alone. Today there are only about 200.

One of the greatest periods of change occurred after the terrible earthquake of August 17, 1959, centered in Montana just west of the west boundary of the park. In the park the earthquake triggered some of the same kinds of convulsions that may have created the park in the first place. There were major alterations in the under-

Old Faithful in winter wraps.

74

ground "plumbing" system. Sapphire Pool, which before only boiled, suddenly started to erupt as a geyser, shooting as high as 175 feet (53.3 meters). Grand Geyser ceased to flow. New mud geysers began to bubble at Sylvan Springs. Massive rock slides tumbled into valleys. Obsidian Cliff split off to a new face and covered the road with black glass. Highways cracked and shifted. Altogether the earthquake caused two million seven hundred dollars of damage to roads, walkways, and buildings in Yellowstone. However, fortunately, no lives were lost in the park.

Steaming pools and springs in the park are almost as interesting as the geysers. Depending on the temperature of the water, the algae grow there in various colors. Grand Prismatic Spring is simply a fairyland of the most brilliant colors, reflected in swirling clouds of steam. Even the little streams running off from Grand Prismatic have banks gleaming in brilliant colors as the temperatures change from hot to cooler.

Some of the small, deep pools have a world reputation for their colors, such as Morning Glory, Opal, and Turquoise pools. Silver Globe Spring takes its name from the large silver bubbles that constantly rise to the surface through its waters.

Mammoth Hot Springs has been called "a mountain turning inside out." Limestone from the inside is brought out and deposited on terraces lining the side of the mountain. Wherever the water is flowing hot, the beautiful colors of the algae cascade down the mountainside. The most incredible stone terraces have been built up with the seeping of the water. Because the water carries limestone and not a harder stone, it builds up very quickly, and new terraces can form in a few months. Objects left in the water are soon coated with limestone.

In various parts of the park are mud volcanoes, fountain "paint pots," where colored earths glurp and plop with eerie noises. Steaming vents roar, or gently steaming vapors keep nearby grass green in the deepest winter.

But the thermal attractions of Yellowstone are not its only features. This undoubtedly would be a national park, even without its geysers and hot springs. One of the world's renowned scenic spots is breathtaking Grand Canyon of the Yellowstone, with its mighty Lower Falls. Anywhere else, smaller Upper Falls would also be a major attraction. Beautiful, vast Yellowstone Lake, Yellowstone River, the multitude of large and small rivers with their beauty and their fishing, Tower Falls, Obsidian Cliff, Electric Peak, the famous and winsome bears, deer, moose, and a host of other animals and birds—all combine to make Yellowstone one of the greatest scenic areas on earth.

"SHEER MAJESTY"

Not content with one of the world's great tourist attractions, Wyoming offers a second, only a short distance from Yellowstone. This is a region so different from Yellowstone it might be on another continent and not 50 miles (80.4 kilometers) away. It is the Grand Teton National Park and Jackson Hole National Monument.

Leaping up from the splendid valley of Jackson Hole, the Tetons radiate with scenery that makes them the most beautiful mountains in America, according to many experts. Here massive Mount Morran is mirrored in the tranquil waters of Jackson Lake. Above all, the stony peak of the Grand Teton soars, and over everything seems to rest a shade of the most magnificent blue color, punctuated by glaciers, gleaming white in clefts on the mountainside. Countless meadows of wild flowers and azure lakes tucked into innumerable basins in the mountainside lure the horseback rider, the hiker, and the nature lover.

Dashing along the base of the Tetons is the "young" Snake River. A float trip down the Snake as far as Moose is one of the major wilderness adventures available to relatively large numbers of people. Cruises on Jackson Lake also lead to hideaways for camp fires and cookouts.

The nation owes thanks to the Rockefeller family for preserving much of the Teton area for all the people, and donating large parts of it to the government for national park purposes.

Jackson Hole with its great elk herd and the picturesque town of

American geography is nowhere more beautifully illustrated than in this scene of majestic Mt. Moran, anchor of the Teton Range, mirrored in tranquil Leigh Lake. Grand Teton National Park treasures some of the world's finest mountain scenery.

77

Jackson are other attractions. Here every summer night visitors may see a true western melodrama re-enacted—the *Hanging of Clover the Killer.*

OTHER NORTHWEST ATTRACTIONS

Memories of America's best-known frontiersman and Western showman abound in the town that bears the last name of "Buffalo Bill" Cody. The fine statue of Buffalo Bill at Cody was created by sculptress Mrs. Harold Payne Whitney. In order to make it completely realistic, she had Bill's favorite horse, Smoky, shipped by express to her studio in New York as the model for the horse on which the statue now is poised in the saddle. Personal items belonging to the showman are displayed in the Buffalo Bill Museum, and there is a frontier ball at Cody on his birthday, called Buffalo Bill Day.

Cody tries to keep the appearance of a frontier Western town. A Trapper's Ball is also held to honor the Sublettes, Colter, and Jim Bridger. The three-day Cody Stampede is one of the country's top rodeos. On these festive occasions, costumed cowboys and cowgirls, in fancy chaps, expensive hats, and high heels, mingle with Indians from the reservation, some wearing bright blankets and often performing dances for the visitors.

Another museum of interest at Cody is the Whitney Gallery of Western Art, where one of the finest collections of such art is assembled. Old timers at Cody like to remember that when the first church was commenced, it was given a "good" start by the poker players at the saloon, who donated the "pot" to the church.

Cowley is a community that revolves strongly around Church Square, the center of Mormon activities. Basin is known for its plantings of trees, said to be among the finest in Wyoming. The Basin region has been known for its bean growing, and the women of Basin have developed a unique art in making pictures and plaques of beans to advertise the region's principal farm product. Basin is especially noted for its rows of beautiful lilacs throughout the town.

The Grand Teton from the Snake River Overlook. The Snake River is part of the Columbia River system. It runs through a canyon by through three mountain ranges. It is then iver. the Salt River and finally flows into the Colum

Hot Springs State Park preserves the world's largest hot medicinal spring—Bighorn Spring, emitting gallons of medicinal water every twenty-four hours. Here are other springs also, and monuments erected by people who claim to have been cured there in such curative places as the Gottsche Rehabilitation Center. There is also a 50-foot (15.2-meter) fall of warm water from the spring and one of the largest and finest terraces, built by lime settling from the spring water.

Great Chief Washakie had a bathhouse at one of the springs here, and the pageant *Gift of Waters* has been given each year since 1925 in memory of Washakie's gift of the springs region to the state. Indians re-enact the ceremony of the presentation. Washakie Fountain is in the park. The Junior Rodeo at Thermopolis is one of the best of its type.

The only Indian reservation in Wyoming today is the great Wind River preserve of the Shoshone and Arapaho. The Indians, particularly the Arapaho, love their ancient ceremonies, and one of the most interesting of these, the continuous seventy-two-hour Sun Dance, can be seen each year.

Fort Washakie is headquarters for the reservation, and here is the grave of the great chief whose name is given to the fort. Here aged Chief Washakie was buried with military honors by the United States. Nearby is said to be the grave of the Indian woman, Sacajawea, who guided Lewis and Clark on their cross-country expedition.

THE SOUTHWEST

A monument at Rendezvous Park near Daniel honors the first two European women to pass through Wyoming—the wives of missionaries Whitman and Spalding. Another monument, near Daniel, shaped like a cruciform granite altar, commemorates the first high mass in Wyoming, conducted by Father Pierre De Smet. Each year a mass is said in memory of this event.

Three thousand elk horns built into an arch across the main street make a spectacular entrance for the town of Afton. Near Afton is an unusual intermittent, or "breathing," spring.

Once South Pass City had a population of two thousand. It is now listed as having fifteen inhabitants. A monument to the visit of missionary Marcus Whitman has been erected there.

Another Western pioneer, Captain John C. Frémont, is honored by a statue at Evanston. Evanston once had a large settlement of Chinese people. Chinese irrigation wheels turned there; there were opium dens and one of the three Chinese joss houses in the United States. The joss house interior was richly carved, beautiful Chinese embroidered draperies decorated the inside, and Chinese residents came from long distances to worship before the idol behind the ornate teakwood screens. The Chinese population dwindled and the joss house burned.

The Green River Rendezvous in Pinedale
is held on the second Sunday in July.

The "Gift of Waters" Pageant in Thermopolis.

Chief Washakie was frequently seen in Evanston, and the treaty creating the Wind River Reservation is on display in the courthouse at Evanston. Near Evanston the primitive frame and stone buildings of historic Fort Bridger have been restored. Between Fort Bridger and Little America, Interstate Highway 80 parallels the Oregon, Mormon, California, and Overland trails, and the route of the picturesque Pony Express. A concrete shaft east of Lyman marks the old Mormon Camp Site.

Rock Springs is known as the "melting pot" of Wyoming because of the forty-seven nationalities who came to make their homes there. International Night is celebrated each May with the people in their native costumes. The railroad operated coal mines there. To defeat a miners' strike, the railroad hired Chinese miners, and Chinatown grew to one thousand two hundred population. In 1875 a mob rushed on Chinatown to burn it, and thirty Chinese were killed, but Chinatown was rebuilt, and Chinese customs, such as New Year celebrations with 100-foot (30.4-meter) dragons and firecrackers, added to the cosmopolitan character of the community.

Northeast of Rock Springs is the desolate Red Desert, where the colors are said to change as regularly as the sun moves.

THE NORTHEAST

The metropolis of northern Wyoming is Sheridan, which began its life on a sheet of brown wrapping paper. The founder of Sheridan, J.D. Loucks, climbed to the crest of a hill. As he tells the story, "The grass was beginning to show green and over across Little Goose was a herd of buffalo ... a small herd of deer was browsing, and as I sat there I was fired with the idea that here was the spot for our city.

"I went home and cooked my supper. After I had eaten I took a sheet of brown wrapping paper and, by the light of a candle, I marked off 40 acres (16 hectares) and laid out a town with streets named after the few settlers. Over the top of the map I wrote 'SHERIDAN' in big letters." The name was in honor of General Phil Sheridan of Civil War fame.

Sheridan began its Wild West show in 1902 by staging a fantastic re-enactment of Custer's Battle of Little Bighorn, which occurred not far away. Two thousand Indians came with their papooses, travois, tepees, and hundreds of dogs to help in staging the fantastic sham battle. A stagecoach filled with prominent guests was overturned when the horses were frightened by the shooting, but the indignant passengers were not hurt. Today the Wyoming Rodeo at Sheridan is said to be the world's largest rodeo of working cowboys.

Each August, All-American Indian Days is celebrated at Sheridan with Indian representatives attending from throughout the country.

Indian arts and crafts are exhibited. There are dances, games, and an Indian Village. The outstanding Indian of the Year is honored, and Miss Indian America is selected.

One of the most unusual museums anywhere is the Bradford Brinton Memorial Ranch, southwest of Sheridan. This is an authentic and faithfully preserved gentleman's working ranch. An outstanding art collection housed at the ranch includes six hundred works of well-known Western artists. Among the most valuable of these is the only known painting of *Custer's Last Stand* by the most famous of all Western artists—Frederic Remington. A blacksmith shop and collection of Western carriages and wagons add to the interest of this unique memorial.

West of Dayton, visitors are startled by the view into 2,000 feet (609.6 meters) deep Tongue River Canyon. Shell Falls is one of the major attractions of the Bighorn Mountains.

Attractions of a wide region of the northeast include: Indian Pow Wow Cavern near Tensleep; Castle Gardens, near Hiland; Fetterman Massacre Monument and Fort Phil Kearny near Buffalo; the Johnson County-Jim Gatchell Memorial Museum at Buffalo; and Teapot Rock, near Midwest. Sundance is the smallest county seat in Wyoming.

There is a legend that two Indian girls once were attacked by bears. They prayed to the great spirit to save them, and he raised the ground where they were standing high into the air. This was one of the many legends of the origin of the unique formation now called Devils Tower. The Indians said the marks on the side of the tower were made by the bears' claws as they scratched along the side. Devils Tower was climbed for the first time in 1893 by a man named Bill Rogers. In 1906 it became our first national monument.

THE SOUTHEAST

Fort Casper was named in honor of Lieutenant Caspar Collins who died in the Platte Bridge fight of 25 army men against 1,600 Indians during the "bloody year on the plains"—1865. Old Fort

Caspar has been restored and offers a museum of pioneer days. (Wyoming's second largest city, Casper, had its name misspelled by a railway clerk's error, and the error was allowed to remain.) The Natrona County Pioneer Museum is housed in the first church built in Casper and shows a fine collection of items used by settlers. The Natrona County gun collection is especially complete. It has one gun bearing eight notches, two of those representing United States marshals.

Near Casper at Bessemer Bend is the first European's cabin built in Wyoming. Hell's Half Acre has been described as a "cave without a roof." The "Register of the Desert," Independence Rock, bears as many as 50,000 names, carved, painted, or scratched into its 190-foot (58-meter) high surface by pioneers, outlaws, trappers, traders, and tourists during more than 115 years of travel.

Whiskey Gap near Bairoil and Lamont was the place where the first enforcement of a liquor prohibition took place. A barrel of whiskey was confiscated and poured on the ground. However, it quickly seeped into the nearby spring, and the demand for spring water grew at a tremendous rate.

The petrified forest east of Route 487 contains subtropical trees of fifty million years ago, which turned to stone.

Douglas is the home of the Wyoming State Fair. On the fairgrounds is the Wyoming Pioneer Museum. At Douglas is the tombstone tribute to the cowboy-rustler, George Pike. Between Douglas and Casper is Ayres Natural Bridge State Park.

Hartville began life as a roaring mining town. The story is told of the gambler, "White Swede," who died at Hartville. Three friends decided to hold his wake. When things grew dull, they agreed on a game of poker and thought it would only be fair to cut the corpse in. By dawn the dead man had "earned" enough in the game to pay for his funeral.

At one time, Lusk was an oil boom town of ten thousand. Now back to a population less than two thousand, it keeps its reminders of early days. Its annual pageant, the *Legend of Rawhide,* is the story of Rawhide Buttes. Lusk Museum contains relics of frontier and stagecoach life.

The massive Guernsey Museum shows the whole life of the

Guernsey area from the time of its prehistoric quarries to the present. Another cliff where names have been carved over the years is Register Cliff near Guernsey. Historic Warm Springs is known as the "Emigrants' Natural Bath Tub of the Plains."

Always one of the key points of the old West, Fort Laramie, or what was left of it, has been preserved as a National Historic Site. Only twenty-one of the original buildings remained. Fortunately, one of these was the post's old Suttler's Store, where Jim Bridger once lived, thought to be the oldest building remaining in Wyoming. Old Bedlam, the officers' quarters, the guardhouse, enlisted men's barracks, cavalry barracks, and other buildings have been restored and considerable effort has been made to give some idea of what Wyoming's oldest permanent settlement looked like in its early days.

In tribute to the sturdy cowboys who passed by Lingle herding longhorns over the Texas Trail, a fine cowboy monument has been erected there.

The Battle Lake region was the scene of an early study of an eclipse by the Henry Draper Astronomical Expedition in 1878. Inventor Thomas Edison accompanied the expedition. The story is told that while fishing with a bamboo rod, Edison got the idea for using bamboo as the filament for his first successful electric light. While this is now considered only a legend, it continues to persist.

In many of Wyoming's sheep herding districts the shepherds occupied their long and lonely hours by piling rocks into tall shafts. These have been called "sheepherders' monuments," and the region around Hanna is one of the best areas in which to find these.

In addition to Fort Laramie, another of Wyoming's communities is named for pioneer trapper Jacques La Ramie. The city of Laramie has outlived its reputation for wildness and now is known as one of the cultural centers of the mountain region. Much of this is due to the influence of the University of Wyoming. Its many fine buildings and museums have much of interest for visitors. Near Laramie is to be seen the world's largest bronze head—the head of Lincoln by University of Wyoming sculptor Robert Russin. The huge work of art weighs 3.5 tons (3.2 metric tons).

Near Laramie is one of the nation's finest but possibly least-

The Lincoln Monument stands on the top of Sherman Hill.

known mountain resort areas—the Snowy Range, sometimes called Medicine Bow Mountains. Between Laramie and Cheyenne grows the famous Tree-in-the-Rock, said to be the most photographed single object in the state.

The gleaming gold leaf dome of the capitol at Cheyenne has stood as a landmark since it was completed in 1890. The Corinthian structure was built of Rawlins sandstone at a total cost of $389,569.13, including the additions of 1915. The fine murals by Allen T. True represent Industry, Pioneer Life, Law, and Transportation. The ceilings of the house and senate chambers are of stained glass, with the state seal in the center.

Wyoming State Museum at Cheyenne displays materials relating to the Indians, ranching, pioneer homes, forts and trails, minerals, and state records. The historical division maintains an unusual collection of archives on Western Americana.

The state capitol in Cheyenne.

Saint Mary's Cathedral at Cheyenne is the largest church in Wyoming.

Every July, during the last week of the month, Cheyenne is transformed by one of the country's largest and best-known annual festivals—Frontier Days, known as "the Daddy of them all." The editor of a Cheyenne newspaper, E.A. Slack, originated the festival in 1897, when three thousand people were on hand. Today, Frontier Days lasts almost a week, with one of the world's most complete and unusual parades, based on the Western theme, dances, and carnivals—and especially the rodeo.

Rodeos in Wyoming are a matter of great civic pride. Many experts consider the Frontier Days rodeo to be the finest in the world. The visitor at Frontier Days receives an insight into the rigors of early Western living, and also realizes that toughness of physique and moral fiber still characterize Wyoming as it looks both backward to the past and forward to the future with all the advantages of an atomic and space age.

Handy Reference Section

Instant Facts

Became the 44th state, July 10, 1890
Capital—Cheyenne, founded 1867
Nickname—The Equality State
State motto— *Equal Rights*
State bird—Meadowlark
State flower—Indian paintbrush
State tree—Cottonwood
State stone—Jade
State symbol—Bucking Horse and Rider (on license plates since 1936)
State song—"Wyoming"
Area—97,203 square miles (251,755 square kilometers)
Rank in area—25th
Greatest length (north to south)—275 miles (443 kilometers)
Greatest width (east to west)—365 miles (587 kilometers)
Highest point—13,804 feet (4,207 meters), Gannett Peak
Lowest point—3,100 feet (945 meters), Belle Fourche River in Crook County
Average altitude—6,700 feet (2,042 meters), second to Colorado
Number of counties—23
Population—374,000 (1970 census)
Population rank—49th
Population density—3 persons per square mile (1 person per square kilometer)
Birthrate—17.2 per 1,000
Physicians per 100,000—105

Principal cities—		
Cheyenne	40,914 (1970 census)
Casper	39,361
Laramie	23,143
Rock Springs	11,657
Sheridan	10,856

You Have a Date with History

1807—John Colter is first known European to enter Wyoming
1811—Wilson Price Hunt expedition crosses Wyoming
1812—Robert Stuart party crosses Wyoming from west to east
1824—First annual fur rendezvous
1828—Antonio Mateo sets up first trading post in Wyoming
1834—First permanent settlement in Wyoming, Fort Laramie
1842—First expedition of John C. Fremont
1843—Second permanent settlement in Wyoming, Fort Bridger
1847—Mormon migrations
1849—California gold rush migrants

1854—Grattan Massacre near Fort Laramie
1860—Pony Express carries messages across Wyoming
1861—Transcontinental telegraph line completed
1863—Bozeman Road established
1866—Fetterman Massacre
1867—Cheyenne founded
1869—Wyoming territory organized; railroad through Wyoming completed across
    continent
1870—Women take first part in public affairs
1872—Yellowstone becomes first of all national parks
1873—Wyoming Stock Growers Association organized
1887—Disastrous winter brought failure to many stockmen
1890—Statehood
1892—Johnson County Cattle War
1897—First Frontier Day at Cheyenne
1902—First National Forest in country established in Wyoming
1906—Devils Tower becomes nation's first National Monument
1924—Nellie Tayloe Ross becomes first woman governor
1929—Grand Teton National Park established
1938—Fort Laramie becomes National Monument (later Historic Site)
1940—Fiftieth anniversary of statehood celebrated across Wyoming
1950—Jackson Hole made a National Monument
1959—Severe earthquake brings major changes to Yellowstone
1965—Diamond jubilee of statehood
1965—Minuteman missile sites completed near Cheyenne
1969—Department of Economic Planning and Development established
1977—Tourism surpasses 10,000,000

Governors of Wyoming

Francis E. Warren, 1890
Amos W. Barber 1890-1893
John E. Osborne 1893-1895
William A. Richards 1895-1899
DeForest Richards 1899-1903
Fenimore Chatterton 1903-1905
Bryant B. Brooks 1905-1911
Joseph M. Carey 1911-1915
John B. Kendrick 1915-1917
Frank Houx 1917-1919
Robert D. Carey 1919-1923
William B. Ross 1923-1924
Frank Lucas 1924-1925
Nellie Tayloe Ross 1925-1927

Frank C. Emerson 1927-1931
Alonzo M. Clark 1931-1933
Leslie A. Miller 1933-1939
Nels H. Smith 1939-1943
Lester G. Hunt 1943-1949
Arthur G. Crane 1949-1951
Frank A. Barrett 1951-1953
C.J. Rogers 1953-1955
Milward L. Simpson 1955-1959
J.J. Hickey 1959-1961
Jack R. Gage 1961-1963
Clifford P. Hansen 1963-1967
Stanley K. Hathaway 1967-1975
Ed Herschler 1975-

Thinkers, Doers, Fighters

People of renown who have been associated with Wyoming

Ashley, William
Beckwourth, Jim
Bridger, Jim
Canary, Martha (Calamity Jane)
Clay, John
Cody, William F. (Buffalo Bill)
Colter, John
Eaton, Alden
Eaton, Howard
Gollings, E.W.
Jackson, David E.
Kendrick, John B.
Kleiber, Hans

McCoy, Tim
Moran, Thomas
Nelson, Avon
Nye, Edgar Watson (Bill)
Red Cloud (Chief)
Penney, J.C.
Pollock, Jackson
Ross, Nellie Tayloe
Sacajawea
Sublette, William
Wister, Owen
Washakie (Chief)

All-American Indian Days in Sheridan.

Index

page numbers in bold type indicate illustrations

Absaroka ("state"), 50
Absaroka Range, 16, 41
Across the Continent (painting), **39**
Afton, 81
Agriculture, 59, 71
Albert, Prince of Monaco, 49
Alcova Lake, 15
All-American Indian Days, 83, **91**
Alpine Junction, 19
Altitude, average, state, 89
American Fur Company, 30
Animals, 53, 54, 71, 76
Arapaho Indians, 24, 26, 31, 42, 50, 80
Area, state, 89
Arikara Indians, 24
Arrow, prehistoric, 23
Arrowheads, 25
Artists, 67, 84
Ashley, William H., 28, 29, 63
Aspen, quaking, 56
Astor, John Jacob, 27, 28
Astoria, OR, 27
Atlantic Creek, 13
Auburn, 60
Authors, 66, 67
Ayres Natural Bridge State Park, 85
Backaboar, 54
Badlands, 19, 20
Bairoil, 85
Baker, Jim, 68
Bannock Indians, 24, 73
Basin (town), 78
Basins, 17, 18, 20
Battle Lake, 86
Beans, 78
Beard, Mrs. Cyrus, 37
Bear River, 14
Bear River Divide, 17
Beaver, 29
Beckwourth, Jim, 29
Belle Fourche River, 19
Benton, 37
Bessemer Bend, 28, 85
Bighorn Basin, 18, 23
Bighorn Mountains, 16, 23, 26, 84
Bighorn River, 14, 18, 27, 64
Bighorn Spring, 80
Big Sandy Lake, 15
Bird, Isabella, 53

Bird, state, 89
Birds, 55
Blackfoot Indians, 24, 63
Black Hills, 16, 26, 61
Blizzards, 22
Block-fault mountains, 20
Blue Holes, 21
Boundaries, state, 13
Boysen Lake, 15
Bozeman, MT, 10
Boseman Trail, 34
Bragg, Bill, Jr., 43
Branding cattle, 44, **45**
Bridger, Jim, 29, 31, 63, 78, 86
Bright, William H., 68
Brinton, Bradford, Memorial Ranch, 84
"Broken Hand," 29
Brundage, George, 47
Buffalo (animals), 15, 26, 31, 39, 53
Buffalo (town), 45, 60, 84
Buffalo Bill Dam, **16**
Buffalo Bill Day, 78
Buffalo Bill Lake, 15
Buffalo Bill Museum, 78
Buffalo Bill Reservoir, 27
Buffalo Bill statue, **65**, 78
Bull Lake, 15
Burntfork, 29
Burt, Struthers, 67
Burt, Mrs. Struthers, 67
Cabin, first in state, 85
Calamity Jane, 66
California gold rush, 32
California Trail, 82
Campbell, John A., 39
Campbell, Robert, 30
Camp Monaco, 49
Canary, Martha (Calamity Jane), 66
Canyons, 19
Capital, territorial, 39
Capitol, state, 67, 87, **88**
Carissa lode, 60
Casper, 60, 85
Castle Gardens, 19, 24, 84
Catholic mass, first, 69, 80
Catlin, George, 52
Cats (Phatty Thompson's), 61, 62
Cattle, **40**, 43-45, **45**, 49, 59
"Cattle Barons," 44
Cattlemen, 44, 45, 49
Central Northern Plains, 20
Charcoal kilns, **58**, 62

Cheyenne, 36, 37, **38**, 39, 46, 48, 53, 61, 62, 67, 72, 87, 88
Cheyenne Indians, 24, 31, 35, 36, 42
Cheyenne *Leader,* 62
Cheyenne River, 14
Chinatown, Rock Springs, 83
Chinese people, 81, 83
Chinook winds, 22
Chittenden, Hiram, 11
Chronology, 89, 90
Chugwater, 44
Church Buttes, 19, 23, 33
Churches, 78, 85, 88
Church Square, Cowley, 78
Cirque lakes, 21
Cities, principal, 89
Civil War, 43
Climate, 22
Cloud Peak, 16
Coal, 57, 60
Cody, William (Buffalo Bill), 49, 64, **65**, 78
Cody (town), 49, 64, **65**, 78
Cody (town), 49, 64, 67, 78
Cody Road, 49
Cody Stampede, 78
Cogly Woo, 54
Colleges, 71
Collins, Caspar, 84
Colorado River, 14
Colter, John, 27, 63, 64, 78
"Colter's Hell," 27
Columbia River, 14, 27, 28, 79
Communication, 62
Community colleges, 71
Como Bluff, 22
Congress, U.S., 36, 39, 42, 47
Continental Divide, 13, 17, 36
Cooper Lake, 15
Copper, 60
Coral reefs, 20
Covered Wagon, The, 66
Cowan, George F., 9-11
"Cowboy Artist," 67
Cowboy monument, 86
Cowley, 78
Cow ponies, 59
Crane, A.G., 71
Crazy Horse (Chief), 65
Crops, 59
Crowheart, 15
Crow Indians, 24
Currier and Ives prints, 25, 28, 34, 39, 48
Custer, George A., 42, 83

Custer's Last Stand (painting), 84
Dakota Territory, 39
Dams, 15, **16**
Daniel (town), 80
Dayton, 59, 84
Deadwood, SD, 46, 61, 62
de Bonneville, B.L.E., 30
Deer Creek, 33
De Smet, Pierre J., 69, 80
Devils Gate, 19, 32
Devils Tower National Monument, 19, 21, 49, 53, 84
Dinosaurs, 22
Divides, 13, 14, 17, 36
Dodge, Grenville M., 36, 37
Douglas, 20, 85
Draper, Henry, Astronomical Expedition, 86
Dry farming, 59
Dubois, 14, 21
Dude ranches, 59, 69
Dull Knife (Chief), 42
Dunraven, Earl of, 42
Earthquake (1959), 73
Eaton brothers, 59
Eclipse (1878), 86
Edison, Thomas, 86
Education, 71, 72
Electric Peak, 76
Elk, 54, **55**, 76
Emigrants Crossing the Plains (painting), **28**
Emigrants' Laundry Tub, 33
"Emigrants' Natural Bath Tub," 86
Encampment (town), 60
Erosion, 59
Evanston, 81, 82
Exploration, 26, 27, 29, 31
Fall, Albert B., 50
Falls, **18**, 76, 80, 84
Farming, 59, 71
Fetterman, W.J., 35
Fetterman Massacre, 35
Fetterman Massacre Monument, 84
Fiftieth anniversary, state, 50
Fish and fishing, 22, 55
Fitzpatrick, Thomas, 29
Flaming Gorge and Dam, 15, 19
Flathead Indians, 24
Floral Valley, 42
Flower, state, 56, 89
Flowers, 55, 56
Foote, Robert, 45

Forests, 49, 56
Fort Bridger, 19, 31, 32, 33, 72, 82
Fort Bridger *Daily Telegraph,* 62
Fort Bridger State Historic Site, 72
Fort Caspar, 84
Fort C.F. Smith, 34
Fort Ellis, 10
Fort John on the Laramie, 30
Fort Laramie, 25, 30, 31, **31,** 32, 33, 34, 35, 48, 53, 71, 86
Fort Laramie National Historic Site, 51, 86
Fort Phil Kearny, 34, 35, 84
Fort Reno, 34
Fort Supply, 33
Fort Washakie, 65, 80
Fort William, 30
Fountain paint pots, 75
Fossil (town), 22
Fossils, 22
Fountain Geyser, 9,10
Frémont, John C., 31, 81
Fremont Lake, 15
Frontier Days, Cheyenne, **38,** 88
Fur trading, 27-30
Gannett Peak, 14, 16
Gas, natural, 60
Gems, 57
Geneva Steel, 60
Geography, 13-20
Geologic Museum, 71
Geology, **11,** 20, 21
Geysers, **8,** 21, 41, 73, **74,** 75
Giant Geyser, 73
Gift of Waters pageant, 80, **82**
Glaciers, 20, 21
Glendo Lake, 15
Gobi Desert, 23
Gold, 32, 37, 60, 61
Gollings, E.W., 67
Goose Creeks, 47, 66, 83
Gottsche Rehabilitation Center, 80
Governors, state, 48, 50, 66, 68, 90
Governors, territorial, 39, 48
Grand Canyon of the Snake River, 19
Grand Canyon of the Yellowstone, The (painting), 67
Grand Canyon of the Yellowstone River, 19, 21, 41, 76
Grand Geyser, 75
Grand Prismatic Spring, 75
Grand Teton, 16, 21, 23, 49, 76, **79**

Grand Teton National Park, **17,** 50, 76
Grant, Ulysses S., 39, 41
Grasses, 55
Grattan, John L., 34
Greasewood, 55
Great Divide Basin, 17
Great Salt Lake, 14
Green River, 14, 29, 61
Green River Lakes, 14
Green River Rendezvous, **81**
Green River Valley, 15, 22
Grey, Zane, 67
Gros Ventre Indians, 24
Gros Ventre Mountains, 17,54
Guernsey, 32, 86
Guernsey Dam, 61
Guernsey Lake, 15
Guernsey Museum, 85
Gulf of California, 14
Gun collection, Natrona County, 85
Gunnysackers, 49
Handcart companies, 32
Hanging of Clover the Killer, 78
Hanna, Oliver, 47
Hanna (town), 86
Harding, Warren G., 50
Hardy, John, 37
Harris, Burton, 27
Hartville, 85
Hattie Lake, 15
Hay, 59
Hayden, F.V., 42, 73
Hayden expedition, 42, 73
Hedges, Cornelius, 41
Helena *Herald,* 41
"Hell on Wheels," 37
Hell's Half Acre, 19, 85
Hickok, Wild Bill, 46, 64
Highest point, state, 16, 89
Highways, 49, 82
Hiland, 22, 84
Hoback, John, 28
Hoback Canyon, 28, 30
"Hole in the Wall" valley, 46
Homesteads, 44
"Horned Dinosaur," 22
Horses, 26, 44, 59
Hot springs, 33, 73, 75, 80
Hot Springs State Park, **12,** 80
Hough, Emerson, 66
Hunt, Wilson Price, 28
Hunting, 54
Idaho, 17
Independence Rock, 19, 85
Indian of the Year, 84
Indian paintbrush, 56
Indian Pow Wow Cavern, 84
Indians, 9, 10, 15, 23, 24-26, 27, 29, 30, 31, 33-36, 39, 42, 43, 50, 60, 64, 65, 69, 80, 83, 84

Indians Attacking the Grizzly Bear (painting), **25**
Indian Village, 84
Industry, 59, 62
International Night, 83
Irma Hotel, Cody, 64
Iron, 60
Irrigation, 59
Isa Lake, 14
Jackson, David E., 29
Jackson, William H., 67
Jackson (town), 78
Jackson Hole National Elk Refuge, 54
Jackson Hole National Monument, 18, 51, 64, 76
Jackson Lake, 15, 76
James Lake, 15
Jenny Lake, 15
Johnson County Cattle War, 44
Johnson County-Jim Gatchell Memorial Museum, 84
Jones, Grant, 54
Joseph (Chief), 9, 43
Joss houses, 81
Junior colleges, 71
Junior Rodeo, 80
Kaycee, 46
K.C. Ranch, 45
Kemmerer, 22, 67
Kendrick, John B., 50, 67
Keyhole Lake, 15
Kiowa Indians, 24
Kleiber, Hans, 67
Lake De Smet, 15
Lakes, 15, 21
Lamont, 19, 85
Lance Creek, 22
Lander, 15, 22, 60
Laning, Edward, 16
La Ramie, Jacques, 68, 86
Laramie, 16, 38, 41, 46, 67, 71, 86
Laramie Mountains, 16, 36
Laramie Peak, 16
Laramie Plains, 20, 43
Laramie River, 15
Legend of Rawhide, 85
Leigh Lake, 15
Length, greatest, state, 89
Lewis and Clark expedition, 64, 80
Limestone, 75
Lime Terrace, Hot Springs State Park, **12**
Lincoln, Abraham, statue of, 86, **87**
Lincoln Highway, 49
Ling fish, 55
Lingle, 86
Lisa, Manuel, 27, 64
Little America (town), 82

Little Big Horn River, 42
Little Missouri River, 14
Little Wolf (Chief), 42
Livestock, 59
Long Trail, 43
"Lore" degrees, 71
Loucks, J.D., 83
Louisiana Purchase, 13
Lower Falls, Yellowstone River, **18,** 76
Lower Geyser Basin, 73
Lowest point, state, 89
Lusk, 85
Lusk Museum, 85
Lyman, 82
Mackenzie, Ranald, 42
"Magic City of the Plains," 37
Magill, Joe, 46
Mammoth Hot Springs, 75
Manufacturing, 62
Manville, 24
Marie Lake, 15
Mateo, Antonio, 29
McCall, Jack, 46
McCoy, Tim, 68
McKinnon, 29
Medicine Bow, 22
Medicine Bow Mountains, 16, 87
Medicine Bow Peak, 16
Medicine Mountain, 23
Medicine Wheel, 23
Meeteetse, 23
Mexican War, 13
Midwest (town), 84
Miles City, MT, 43
Minerals and mining, 57, 59-61
Mines, "lost," 60
Mirror Lake, 15
Miss Indian America, 84
Missouri River, 14
Modoc Indians, 24
Molly Island, 55
Monroe, W.N., 37
Montana, 9, 10, 34, 43, 73
Moorcroft, 68
Moore, Olga, 47
Moose (town), 76
Moraines, 21
Moran, Thomas, 67
Mormon Camp Site, 82
Mormons, 32, 33, 59, 78
Mormon Trail, 61, 82
Morning Glory Pool, 75
Morris, Esther Hobart, 66
Motion pictures, 69
Motto, state, 89
Mountain lion, **56**
Mountains, 16, 17, 20, 21
Mount Moran, **17,** 67, 76, **77**
Mud volcanoes, 75
Murals, Capitol, 87

93

Museums, 71, 78, 84, 85, 86, 87
My Life on the Range, 67
National forests, 49, 56
National historic site, 51, 86
National monuments, 49, 51, 76, 84
National parks, **17,** 42, 50, 75, 76
National Park Service, 53
Natrona County Pioneer Museum, 85
Natural gas, 60
Natural Resources Board, 57
Nelson, Avon, 71
"Nesters," 44
Nevada, 17
Newcastle, 60
Newspapers, 62
Nez Percé Creek, 10
Nez Percé Indians, 9, 10, 24, 43
Nickname, state, 89
Niobrara River, 14
NODE (town), 44
North Platte River, 14, 31, 50, 61, 68
Nye, Edgar Watson (Bill), 67
Obsidian, 25, 63
Obsidian Cliff, 63, 75, 76
Oil, 50, 57, 59, 60, 85
Olay, John, 67
Old Bedlam, Fort Laramie, 86
Old Faithful geyser, **8,** 41, 73, **74**
Old Main building, University of Wyoming, **70**
Opal Pool, 75
Ore processing, 61
Oregon, 9, 17, 27
Oregon Territory, 13
Oregon Trail, 28, 30, 32, 61, 66, 82
Organic Act of Wyoming, 39
Osage, 22
Outlaws, 46
Overland Trail, 61, 82
Owl Creek Range, 19
Pacific Creek, 13
Parker, Samuel, 30
Parks, **12, 17,** 42, 50, 75, 76, 80, 85
Pathfinder Lake, 15
Pelicans, 55
Penney, J.C., 67, **68**
Petrified forest, 22, 63, 85
Petroglyphs, 24
Petroleum, 50, 57, 59, 60, 85
Petrotomics, 61
Phillips, John (Portugee), 35
Pictographs, 24
Piedmont, 58
Pike, George, 85

Pine Bluffs, 43
Pinedale, 69, 81
Pioneering, 47
Pioneer's Home (painting), **48**
Plains regions, 20
Plants, 55, 56, 71
Polecat Bench, 22
Pollock, Jackson, 67
Pony Express, 61, 64, 82
Population figures, 37, 47, 89
Pools, hot, 75
Popo Agie River, 15
Powder River, 14, 29, 65
Powder River (book), 67
Powell, James, 36
Powell (town), 22
Prairie dogs, **52,** 53
Prairie Dog Town (painting), **52**
Precipitation, 22
Prehistoric times, 20, 21, 23, 24
Presidents, U.S., 39, 41, 49, 50, 66
Ptarmigan Mountain, 16
Quaking aspen, 56
Quarries, 24, 25, 71
Radersburg, MT, 9
Railroads, 36-39, 60, 61, 64
Rainbow Canyon, 19
Ranches and ranching, 44, 45, 49, 59, 84
Rawhide Buttes, 85
Rawlins, 22, 31, 46, 60
Rawline red (paint color), 60
Rawlins sandstone, 87
Red Canyon, 42
Red Cloud (Chief), 34, 35, 36, 65
Red Desert, 17, 83
Reed, Marshal, 47
Register Cliff, 32, 86
"Register of the Desert," 85
Regulators, 45
Remington, Frederic, 84
Rendezvous, trappers, 29, 30, 63
Rendezvous Park, 80
Reservations, Indian, 50, 69, 80
"River of the Yellow Stone," 14
Rivers, 14, 15
Riverton, 61
Roberts, John, 69
Rockefeller family, 76
Rock Hound clubs, 57
Rock Springs, 20, 60, 61, 82
Rocky Mountain Herbarium, 71
Rocky Mountains, 22
Rocky Mountain sheep, 54
Rodeos, 44, 78, 80, 83, 88

Rogers, Bill, 84
Roosevelt, Franklin Delano, 66
Roosevelt, Theodore, 49
Ross, Nellie Tayloe, 50, 66
Roundups, 44
Russin, Robert, 86
Rustlers, 44, 45
Sacajawea, 80
Sage, 55
Sage grouse, 55
Saint Mary's Cathedral, 88
Salt, 60
Salt Creek Oil Field, 60
Salt River Range, 17
Sandstone, **11,** 71, 87
Sapphire pool, 75
Savery, 68
Schoolhouse, first, 71, **72**
Schools, 69, 71, 72
Semi-Centennial Geyser, 73
Seminoe Lake, 15
Seminoe Range, 17
Senators, U.S., 50, 68
Seventy-fifth anniversary, state, 51
Shaughnessy, John, 37
Sheep, 49, 54, 59, 86
Sheepeater Indians, 24
Sheepherders' monuments, 86
Sheepmen, 49
Shell Canyon, 19
Shell Creek, 72
Shell Falls, 84
Shelter belts, 57
Sheridan, Phil, 83
Sheridan (city), 15, 22, 23, 50, 60, 66, 83, 91
Sheridan *Post-Enterprise,* 47
Sheridan Valley, 18
Sherman Hill, 37, 87
Shoshone Canyon, 19
Shoshone Indians, 24, 26, 50, 64, 65, 69, 80
Shoshone Lake, 15
Shoshone mission boarding school, 69
Shoshone reservation, 69
Shoshoni, 24
Sierra Madre Range, 17
Silver Globe Spring, 75
Silver Lake, 15
Sinclair, Harry F., 50
Sinclair Oil Company, 50
Sioux Indians, 24, 26, 33, 35, 36
Slack, E.A., 88
Smoky (horse), 78
Snake River, 14, 19, 64, 76, 79
Snow, E.P., 37
Snowfalls, 22
Snowshoes, Indian, 25

Snowy Range, 15, 16, 56, 87
Snowy Range Nature Area, 71
Soapstone quarries, 25
Soda ash, refining, 61
South Dakota, 26, 46, 61
South Pass, 28, 30, 60, 66
South Pass City, 37, 81
Spalding, Henry H., 30, 80
Spanish-American War, 49
"Spanish Diggings," 24
Spanish in Wyoming, 24, 26
Springs, hot, 33, 73, 75, 80
Stagecoaches, 61
Stamp, 50th anniversary of state, 50
Star Dust (Indian), 15
Star Valley, 33
State Historical Society, 61
Statehood, 47-48
State parks, **12,** 80, 85
Statistics, state, 89
Steamboat, 61
Stone, state, 89
Stonehenge, 23
Stringer, Samuel, 63
Stuart, Robert, 28
Sublette, William, 29, 78
Sublette, William L., 30, 78
Sundance (town), 84
Sun Dances, Indian, 26, 80
Sunrise (town), 60
Suttler's Store, Fort Laramie, 86
Swan, Alexander H., 44
Sylvan Springs, 75
Symbols, state, 89
Taking the Back Track (painting), **34**
T.A. Ranch, 45
Teapot Dome scandal, 50
Teapot Rock, 84
Ten Eyck, Tenadore, 35
Tensleep (town), 25, 84
Tensleep Canyon, 19
Tensleep Creek, 19
Tepee rings, 24
Teton Mountains, 15, 16, 18, 20, 21, 27, **51,** 56, 64, 67, 76
Teton Pass, 27, 28
Teton uplift, 20
Texas annexation, 13
Texas Trail, 43, 86
Thermal activity, 27, 73, 75
Thermopolis, 46, 80, 82
Thompson, Phatty, 61, 62
Thompson, William (Big Bill), 68
Timber, 56
Tongue River, 14
Tongue River Canyon, 84
Torrey Lake, 25
Torrington, 28
Tower Falls, 76

Trading, 27-29
Trading post, first, 29
Transcontinental railroad, 36-39, 61
Transportation, 61, 62
Trapper's Ball, Cody, 78
Trapping, 28-30
Tree, state, 89
Tree-in-the-Rock, 87
Trees, 56, 78
Trees, petrified, 22, 63, 85
Trona, 61
Trout, 55
True, Allen T., 87
Tump Range, 17
Turquoise Pool, 75
Two Bar Cattle Company, 44
Two Ocean Pass, 13
Universities, 71
University of Wyoming, **70**, 71, 86
Union Pacific Railway, 36
Upper Falls, Yellowstone River, 76
U.P. Trail, 67

Uranium, 61
Utah, 15, 17, 32, 33
Ute Indians, 24
UVA (town), 44
Valleys, 18
Vaux, William, 71
Verendrye brothers, 26
Vigilantes, 46
Virginian, The, 66
Volcanoes, 20, 21
"Wagon Box" fight, 36
Waltman, 19
Wapiti Range, 17
Warm Springs, 33, 86
Warren, Francis E., 48
Washakie (Chief), 64, 80, 82
Washakie Fountain, 80
Washburn, Henry, 41
Washburn-Langford-Doane party, 41
Waterfalls, **18**, 76, 80, 84
Watersheds, 13, 14
Water sources, 57
Webster, Daniel, 13
Wheatland Lake, 15

Whiskey Gap, 85
Whitehawk (Indian), 73
Whitehead, J.R., 36
"White Swede," 85
Whitman, Marcus, 30, 63, 80, 81
Whitney, Mrs. Harold Payne, 78
Whitney Gallery of Western Art, 78
Width, greatest, state, 89
Wild flowers, 55, 56
William, King of Prussia, 41
Wind River, 14, 64
Wind River Canyon, 19
Wind River Glacier, 20
Wind River Range, 16, 21, 60
Wind River Reservation, 50, 80, 82
Wind River Wilderness, 20
Wister, Owen, 66
Wolf Creek, 59
Wolves, 54
Women's rights, 41, 50, 66, 68
Woodruff, J.D., 13

Wool, 59
World War I, 50, 59
World War II, 51
Wyoming Pioneer Museum, 85
Wyoming Rodeo, 83
Wyoming State Fair, 85
Wyoming State Museum, 87
Wyoming *State Tribune*, 62
Wyoming Stock Growers Association, 59, 68
Wyoming Territory, 39, 46
Yankton, SD, 39
Yellowstone Forest Reserve, 49
Yellowstone Lake, 15, 21, 41, 55, 76
Yellowstone National Park, 9, 11, 14, 22, 24, 25, 27, 29, 41, 42, 43, 49, 50, 53, 54, 55, 63, 64, 73-76
Yellowstone River, 14, **18**, 19, 28, 76
Yellowstone River Company, 64

PICTURE CREDITS

ABOUT THE AUTHOR

With the publication of his first book for school use when he was twenty, **Allan Carpenter** began a career as an author that has spanned more than 135 books. After teaching in the public schools of Des Moines, Mr. Carpenter began his career as an educational publisher at the age of twenty-one when he founded the magazine *Teachers Digest*. In the field of educational periodicals, he was responsible for many innovations. During his many years in publishing, he has perfected a highly organized approach to handling large volumes of factual material: after extensive traveling and having collected all possible materials, he systematically reviews and organizes everything. From his apartment high in Chicago's John Hancock Building, Allan recalls, "My collection and assimilation of materials on the states and countries began before the publication of my first book." Allan is the founder of Carpenter Publishing House and of Infordata International, Inc., publishers of *Issues in Education* and *Index to U. S. Government Periodicals*. When he is not writing or traveling, his principal avocation is music. He has been the principal bassist of many symphonies, and he managed the country's leading non-professional symphony for twenty-five years.

96